While Reading Through John's Gospel
- 1 -

While Reading Through John's Gospel
- 1 -
BE Yoo
ISBN-13: 978-1-60668-007-0
ISBN-10: 1-60668-007-2
Copyright © 2007, Evangelical Media Group, Inc.
Printed in U.S.A.
No part of this book may be reproduced
without permission from the publisher.

While Reading Through John's Gospel
- 1 -

B.E. Yoo

Evangelical Media Group

◆ Explanatory Notes

1. The King James Version of the Bible is used in this book unless indicated otherwise.

2. This is the first of a series of books based on 55 sermons. (Originally, there were 56 sermons but two of them were combined as one.) Each sermon was originally about two hours long.

3. The speaker approached John's Gospel in chronological order, focusing each sermon on a specific passage.

4. After each sermon, the speaker and a team of editors spent time reviewing the content of the sermons.

◆ Foreword

While Reading Through John's Gospel

It might be said that John's Gospel focuses strongly on spiritual matters, and the other three Gospels present accounts of many of Jesus' teachings and physical activities. Matthew and Luke's Gospels, for example, contain detailed accounts of the events surrounding Jesus' birth, while John's Gospel does not even mention His birth.

John's Gospel, however, explains more powerfully than the other three Gospels what kind of personage Jesus was. The very first verse tells us, "In the beginning was the Word, and the Word was with God, and the Word was God" John 1:1. It announces precisely that Jesus was the Word that has existed from the beginning, and at the same time, He was God. So we might say that Matthew, Mark, and Luke's Gospels concentrate more on Jesus' physical actions, while John's Gospel focuses on Jesus' mind, in other words, His thoughts. In John chapter 20 verse 31, the apostle John expressed very clearly his purpose in writing this Gospel:

> "But these are written, that ye might believe that Jesus is the Christ, the Son of God; and that believing ye might have life through his name."

Also, in John chapter 5 verse 39 it says, "[You] Search the scriptures; for in them ye think ye have eternal life: and they are they which testify of me." The apostle John wrote that his reason for recording John's Gospel was so that we, as individuals, might have eternal life. The Bible is different from any other book in the world in that it deals with the matter of eternal life, that is, the matter of the human spirit. As we draw near to the Bible, we are able to examine matters that are related to our lives, and more specifically, our spirits. For this reason, when we read the Bible, it should be with the most sincere of hearts.

Which is the most precious book ever written in the history of mankind? People sometimes describe a piece of writing as being "a real gem" but is there any literary gem more precious than the words of the Bible? Aren't there times when a Bible verse that you have read many times before suddenly takes on a new meaning for you, giving you a peace in your spirit that nothing in this world could give to you?

There is no book that can compare to the Bible. When you read other books, they offer little more than the experience of climbing a bare mountain. The Bible, however, gives the reader that feeling of being deep in the mountains, eager to climb and explore. From a distance, all you may see is a mountain ridge, but the deeper you go in amongst the mountains, the more you discover: valley after valley, countless trees, streams, and rocks. The same is true of the Bible. No matter how many times you may read the Bible, it will seem different every time. The content remains the same, but each time you read it, you see it from a different perspective. So, when you approach the Bible, you should examine it thoroughly, bearing in mind that it is a real treasure.

The Bible describes the conception of the nation of Israel. The seed of this nation fell to the ground and as descendants were born, they were planted in the land that God had promised them. A nation was established in that land, that nation became stronger, and at times the members of that nation had to endure tremendous hardships. God called Abraham, the forefather of that nation, and commanded him, saying, "Get thee out of thy country, and from thy kindred, and from thy father's house, unto a land that I will shew thee" Genesis 12:1. Abraham put his trust in these words of God and set out on his journey. Later, he again believed God's words of promise and as a result, he was given a son, Isaac, to be his heir. Abraham's life continued step by step, just as it says in Romans chapter 1 verse 17: "For therein is the righteousness of God revealed from faith to faith." Little by little, the fellowship that Abraham had with God became deeper, as he advanced from faith to faith towards the land of Canaan. In our case, too, as we draw near to the Bible, we come to discover Jesus Christ, just as the Bible tells us: "So then faith cometh by hearing, and hearing by the word of God" Romans 10:17. Also, Jesus was born through the word of God. He came in accordance with the words of the Old Testament, and He died and rose again from the dead in accordance with these same words. This is why we also take pride in having been born of God's word. It is only through the words of the Bible that a person's spirit is born again. Doesn't the Bible say that God "begat . . . us with the word of truth" James 1:18? Without God's word, we could not be born as citizens of the kingdom of God. This is why we need to keep close to the words of the Bible with childlike hearts and be able to look to Jesus Christ.

The words of the Bible are the words of God and they are as alive today as they were at the time of Abraham, the father of faith, and at any other time in history. Also, the words of the Bible wield the power to be able to take hold of the spirit and heart of any individual during their life in this world and guide them until they come to stand before the Lord. Since the One who has boarded the same boat as we are on has said, "Let us go over unto the other side" Luke 8:22, since He has determined our destination and His words are alive, we must not forget His words when we face the storms of this world.

The reason I am saying all this before we commence our study of John's Gospel is that I earnestly hope that through these studies, we may be able to come closer to God's word and thus be able to overcome the many worries, anxieties, and hardships of this world. All we need to do is allow God's word to be the light that guides us through our lives, as it says in the book of Psalms: "Thy word is a lamp unto my feet, and a light unto my path" Psalm 119:105.

When Peter looked to Jesus as He was walking on the water, Peter was also able to stand on the water. When a storm arose shortly after this, however, Peter looked at the waves with fear and began to sink. When we first came to know the gospel and believed firmly in the love of Jesus Christ, we floated above all the storms of the world. Our hearts definitely stood above the storm and were not pulled down into it. As we continue to live in this turbulent world, however, the time comes when we become aware that we are beginning to sink. Our lives become increasingly sluggish.

When Jesus came to this world and before He began His public ministry, He experienced something that was also intended as a lesson for us. As the devil tempted Him to turn some stones into bread, Jesus replied, "Man shall not live by bread alone, but by every word that proceedeth out of the mouth of God" See Matthew 4:3-4. He said these words at a time when He himself was suffering from extreme hunger.

Even though we know in theory that the words of the Bible are food for our spirits, if we are not careful, we may easily forget to apply these words to our actual lives. So as we deal with the matters of our lives in this world, we need to form a habit of using every spare moment to read the Bible so that whenever and wherever we sit down we think about reading the Bible.

In the Psalms it says, "Blessed is the man that walketh not in the counsel of the ungodly, nor standeth in the way of sinners, nor sitteth in the seat of the scornful. But his delight is in the law of the Lord; and in his law doth he meditate day and night" Psalm 1:1-2. As we are living in this world, we should always chew over God's word thoroughly and trust in His word in our hearts. Love is always a matter of give and take. We become aware of God's love through His word so shouldn't we also demonstrate our love for God by obeying His word in our lives?

The only truth is Jesus Christ who is in the Bible. If you do not know Jesus Christ, all you are doing is stepping on mere shadows of the truth. Jesus said, "I am the way, the truth, and the life: no man cometh unto the Father, but by me" John 14:6. There is no other way than this. So the Bible says, "There is a way which seemeth right unto a man, but the end thereof are the ways of death" Proverbs 14:12, and Jesus said, "Enter ye in at the strait gate" Matthew 7:13.

As you are reading the Bible, you may often find that verses come to mind other than the ones you are reading. There are many times when I am reading John's Gospel and other verses flash through my mind, so I look up these verses and read that part of the Bible for a while. Sometimes while I am reading John's Gospel, I turn to the book of Jeremiah and read that, or Isaiah, or Genesis. This is because I find I understand John's Gospel better by reading these other books as well. The mysteries of the Bible are only unraveled by other passages from the Bible.

The apostle John actually met and touched the One who was the Word. There was something that he knew for certain. This was why he wrote, "That which was from the beginning, which we have heard, which we have seen with our eyes, which we have looked upon, and our hands have handled, of the Word of life" 1 John 1:1. It is the testimony of this apostle John that we read in John's Gospel. Through John's Gospel, the apostle testifies as to who Jesus Christ was. Who is this Jesus in whom we believe? It is the Jesus that appears in John's Gospel.

The content of John's Gospel is of a higher dimension. It deals with magnificent and grandiose matters, not of this earth but of heaven above. So, as we study John's Gospel, we may see this as a time to lay ourselves a firm foundation in God's word. Once we have finished a thorough study of John's Gospel, it will probably be easier to understand other parts of the Bible.

We should see our studies of John's Gospel as an opportunity to be able to understand the Bible more easily; we should not think that once we have studied John's Gospel there will be no need to study the Bible any more. There is in fact no end to studying the Bible. It is my hope that those who hear and read the content of this book will see in it not the writer, but Jesus Christ alone. I also hope that His words and His words alone remain in the hearts and minds of my readers.

◆ Index

1	The Word of Eternal Life John 1:1-3	15
2	From Life to Eternal Life John 1:4-5	29
3	The Light of Lights John 1:6-18	51
4	The Lamb of God, Who Taketh Away the Sin of the World John 1:19-42	75
5	Those Who Followed Jesus John 1:43-51	95
6	The Wedding to Which Jesus was Invited John 2:1-11	121
7	Jesus and the Temple John 2:12-25	149
◆	Notes	174

1

The Word of Eternal Life

John 1:1-3

God created the heaven and the earth through His word.
His plan and His purpose were contained in His word.
God created man in His own image
in order to pour out His word into man's heart
and entrust His word to man.

John 1:1-3

¹In the beginning was the Word, and the Word was with God, and the Word was God.

²The same was in the beginning with God. ³All things were made by him; and without him was not any thing made that was made.

The World Knew Him Not

There is a course of events that flows through the Bible, guided by a certain power that cannot be expressed in human terms. Beginning with the colossal work of the creation, the universe came into being and the history of mankind has unfolded according to the master plan of the Creator. Within the course of that history, one Person, the very essence of that power, came to this earth in the body of a man. Even though this Creator Himself appeared in this way, people did not recognize who He was.

Perhaps I can illustrate this point with an example. Imagine someone taking a photograph of a very large group of people lined up in rows on some steps. In order to capture the entire group, the photographer would have to stand back quite a distance. Without a doubt, the camera would capture the full scene, but you would not be able to recognize each individual.

In a similar way, people were not able to recognize the Creator when He appeared in the history of mankind.

The Creator Appeared in the Course of History

After He had created the heavens and the earth, the One who has the power of creation chose one area of land on the tiny planet Earth in the midst of the vast universe, and here He made man from the dust of the ground. This man did not evolve from the amoeba to the monkey, and on to the human form, as the evolutionists would have us believe. In the course of the history of mankind, countless people have been born and died. Even now, people are living and dying. Since God made man out of the dust of the ground, man returns to the dust of the ground.

When I consider the hand of God stretched out over all things in the universe that He created, I am reminded of the words of a hymn.

> O, Lord my God! When I in awesome wonder
> Consider all the worlds Thy hands have made,
> I see the stars, I hear the rolling thunder,
> Thy pow'r throughout the universe displayed.
> Then sings my soul, My Savior God to Thee;
> How great Thou art, how great Thou art![1]

This great God who established the universe chose this tiny Earth amongst the many stars and planets, and here He set in action the series of events that make up the history of mankind. In the course of this history, one special person came into the world. There is a hymn that describes God's love.

> It goes beyond the highest star,
> And reaches to the lowest hell.[2]

It was this God, the Creator of the universe and all things in it, who one day came to the earth to participate in the history of mankind. Sometimes I am amazed at how fortunate I am to have come to believe in God. How was I able to come to know the name of God in a world such as ours? He came into this world for the sake of mankind, these pathetic and worthless beings. The mere thought of this leaves my heart too full for words.

God the Father, God the Son, and God the Holy Spirit

John chapter 1 verse 1 reads:

"In the beginning was the Word, and the Word was with God, and the Word was God."

Then in verse 2, it says:

"The same was in the beginning with God."

We can take these two verses as forming one paragraph, can't we? One day as I was reading this text, it struck me that the way it has been recorded is really quite remarkable. How many times does the expression, "the Word," appear in this passage? It is used three times. And how many times does the word, "God," appear? It is also used three times, isn't it? There is an important passage in the Old Testament that also refers to God three times. This was when God created man.

"And God said, Let us make man in our image, after our likeness."
Genesis 1:26

"Us," or the possessive form "our," appears here three times, doesn't it? "Let us make man in our image, according to our likeness." What kind of God is it that we believe in? What do we believe Him to be like? We believe in God the Father, God the Son, and God the Holy Spirit, don't we? This passage from John's Gospel would appear to be the finest expression of God's triunal nature.

If the Word Had Not Been There in the Beginning

What would have happened if there had been something else instead of the Word in the beginning? Suppose there had been some huge, magnificent being in the beginning instead of the Word. If that had been the case, it would have died and decomposed a long time ago. You can be sure that it would have long since ceased to exist.

Here in John chapter 1 verse 1, however, it clearly says:

"In the beginning was the Word."

The Bible also tells us that God is "upholding all things by the word of his power" Hebrews 1:3.

In John chapter 1 verse 3 it says, "All things were made by him; and without him was not any thing made that was made" John 1:3. The Bible also says, "By the word of the Lord were the heavens made; and all the host of them by the breath of his mouth" Psalm 33:6, and, "Through faith we understand that the worlds were framed by the word of God" Hebrews 11:3.

Furthermore, the Bible tells us clearly:

"Till heaven and earth pass, one jot or one tittle shall in no wise pass from the law, till all be fulfilled," Matthew 5:18

and that

"Heaven and earth shall pass away, but my words shall not pass away." Matthew 24:35

The Bible speaks for God, since the Word is God. So it is through the words recorded in the Bible that we gradually come to know God. In our lives, there are certain objects that we are acquainted with but do not really know. Let's take a microphone as an example. This is a familiar object, but at the same time we do not necessarily know what is inside it, do we? But there are certain people who know. A person who has taken a microphone apart and put it back together again and the person who designed the microphone will know all about it. No matter how complex a man-made object may be, if you ask the designer, he will be able to tell you all about it.

There is also Someone who created the universe and He knows what He wants and what His aim is. No matter how widely man may try to investigate the universe, however, he will never be able to know everything about it. So God created the earth and then He sent His Son to this earth that He had created in order to explain to mankind His purpose and His will. The Bible was recorded in order to explain all about God's Son, His reason for sending Him into the world, and how His Son will come again to take us with Him to our final destination.

Since this is the case, how is this Word operating in this world? The fact that God began all things by His word is extremely important. When God created everything in the universe, He started all things through His word; this world did not come into being through any physical form or shape. If God had not begun all things through His word, we would not be able to believe in Him. How could we possibly believe in Him?

Sometimes we get frustrated as we try to understand other people's thoughts and in the end we tell them to, "Just say it!" Words are an expression of thoughts. If we speak without thinking, there is a greater possibility of miscommunication. If our thoughts are clear, however, our words will also flow clearly and smoothly, and we will be able to converse with other people effectively.

There Were Thoughts Behind the Words

If we consider the significance of "the Word" a little more deeply, we find that it contains God's plan, His purpose, and His will. In other words, the Word contains God's thoughts. He gave the commands through His Word in accordance with His thoughts and in this way, He created all things. So the Bible says, "All things were made by him."

Let's think of it this way. A person who has a purpose and a plan can visualize what he wants to achieve even if no one else can understand what he is aiming at. Imagine an architect standing on an empty piece of land. As he looks around him, he is designing something in his head and he can visualize the final structure in his mind. A person standing next to him will not be able to see this, and might ask him what he is doing, but as the architect stands there in the open field, he can see with his mind's eye what kind of house he wants to build there and what it will look like inside and out. All these details arise from his thoughts. The house cannot just come into existence on its own. It all comes from his mind. If you carefully examine a plant, or a tree, or some other product of nature, you will find that there are profound laws hidden within it and that it did not just appear without plan or purpose.

The idea that all things just happened to come into being by chance is simply a theory that some scientists have come up with.

"All things were made by him, and without him was not any thing made that was made." John 1:3

In Genesis chapter 1 it says, "In the beginning God created the heaven and the earth" Genesis 1:1, and in John chapter 1, "In the beginning was the Word, and the Word was with God, and the Word was God" John 1:1. Here we can see that God the Father, God the Son, and God the Holy Spirit were working together.

In Proverbs chapter 8 we find the verse that says, "Then I was beside Him, as a master workman; and I was daily His delight, Rejoicing always before Him" Proverbs 8:30 NASV.

"The Lord possessed me in the beginning of his way, before his works of old. I was set up from everlasting, from the beginning, or ever the earth was. When there were no depths, I was brought forth; when there were no fountains abounding with water. Before the mountains were settled, before the hills was I brought forth: while as yet he had not made the earth, nor the fields, nor the highest part of the dust of the world. When he prepared the heavens, I was there: when he set a compass upon the face of the depth: when he established the clouds above: when he strengthened the fountains of the deep: when he gave to the sea his decree, that the waters should not pass his commandment: when he appointed the foundations of the earth: then I was by him, as one brought up with him: and I was daily his delight, rejoicing always before him; rejoicing in the habitable part of his earth; and my delights were with the sons of men."

Proverbs 8:22-31

Who is this talking about? It is Jesus, God the Son, the Word who became flesh and dwelt among us. He was at God's side as the Creator and was daily His delight, rejoicing in His habitable world, and His delight was with the sons of men.

God had the words of the Bible recorded in order to provide hope and joy to all of mankind, born into this world and destined to die. It was this same Word of God that created the heaven and the earth.

The Creation: the Foundation upon which the Word Would Be Given as a Blessing to Man

When someone has a purpose, he also needs a setting in which to carry it out. God had a purpose and in order to carry it out, the earth had to be formed, there needed to be life on that earth, and a course of events had to unfold. What could God give to man in an empty space?

Suppose you are walking through a desert, almost dying from thirst and exhaustion. Then a helicopter flies by and the pilot shouts out, "Here! Have some water! I'll pour out a gallon for you and then I'm off!" Would you be able to take the water and drink it? You might just catch a few drops in your cupped hands, but that would be all, and it would not be enough to quench your thirst. What would be the point in a whole gallon of water being poured out? If you did not have a container in which to catch it, the water would just soak into the ground.

God embarked on the creation of the world through His Word in order to establish a foundation, or container, so that He might give His Word to mankind, and bestow His blessings on man, thus fulfilling man's needs. Perhaps this was what inspired one believer in the past to write the words of this hymn:

> All creatures of our God and King
> Lift up your voice and with us sing.
> Alleluia, Alleluia![3]

All creatures of our God and King, all creatures under the heavens, praise the Lord! These are no ordinary words. God was looking for vessels that could be filled with His word and thus be able to praise His name, but could He have progressed towards this aim without first making the land on which the people who were to receive His word would be able to live? So God formed man in His own image as a vessel into which He might pour out His word. He wanted to entrust His word to man, so He created man out of the dust of the ground in order to give him His word. He wanted to fill man with His word so that He might communicate with man heart to heart.

There Was Nowhere for God's Word to Be Received

What was the first request that God made to man who had thus been created in God's likeness? Let's read the passage that contains this request.

> "Of every tree of the garden thou mayest freely eat: But of the tree of the knowledge of good and evil, thou shalt not eat of it: for in the day that thou eatest thereof thou shalt surely die." Genesis 2:16-17

God laid down a law for man at the beginning. He told Adam that he was free to eat from any of the trees in the garden except for one;

he was forbidden to eat from the tree of the knowledge of good and evil.

This was the first conversation God had with man. Adam could eat any of the fruits of the garden except for the fruit of the tree of the knowledge of good and evil. Adam heard these words of God, but there was no room for them in his heart. If he had truly accepted these words, he might not have eaten the forbidden fruit. Even after Adam had heard God's words, however, he still ate some of the fruit from the tree of the knowledge of good and evil. In doing so, he made a terrible mistake. God's word no longer had a place in man's heart because man had rejected it. God should have been resting, but as soon as man sinned, God had to start working again. How did He go about this?

In Genesis chapter 1 verse 1 it says:

"In the beginning God created the heaven and the earth."

It goes on to describe how He created all things and then He rested on the seventh day. But then man sinned. Many years later, God commanded Abraham, saying, "Go to the land that I will show you."

> "Get thee out of thy country, and from thy kindred, and from thy father's house, unto a land that I will shew thee." Genesis 12:1

Abraham listened to these words and departed accordingly. Then, "Abraham begat Isaac; and Isaac begat Jacob; and Jacob begat Judas and his brethren; And Judas begat Phares and Zara of Thamar; Phares begat Esrom; and Esrom begat Aram" Matthew 1:2-3.

As the family line continued in this way, the history of the Jews unfolded, and God repeatedly spoke to man through this history over a long period of time.

My Father Worketh Hitherto, and I Work

Then one day, a certain person suddenly came to a particular land. It was the land to which God had sent Abraham long after Adam had sinned and had been expelled from the Garden of Eden. This was the land that would become Israel. There Abraham settled and there his descendants were born generation after generation as history flowed down to the time of Jesus. At one time, the Israelites were driven out of their land and were taken as captives into foreign lands. Later, after they returned to their land, they were conquered by another nation. It was while this nation was in control that Jesus was born.

One day as Jesus was walking, He came across a boisterous crowd of people with physical ailments, pushing their way towards a pool called Bethesda. One man, however, was simply lying on his mat watching. He was a paralytic and did not even try to join in. Jesus asked him:

"Wilt thou be made well?"

And the man answered:

"Sir, I have no man to put me into the pool."

In those days, an angel of the Lord would go down and stir up the waters of the pool called Bethesda. Whoever stepped in first was cured of his affliction. This story is told in John's Gospel chapter 5. This man had been lying near the pool for 38 years. He had no one to put him in the waters so all he could do was lie there. When Jesus came by, He told the man to take up his mat and walk, and immediately the paralytic was healed. It is quite amazing, but this paralytic simply believed Jesus' words, stood up, and walked. It was the Sabbath day when Jesus performed this miracle, so the Jews began to criticize Him, but what did Jesus say in response to this?

"My Father worketh hitherto, and I work."   John 5:17

God created man but ever since man sinned, God has been carrying out the task of saving mankind. This is what Jesus meant when He said, "My Father worketh hitherto, and I work." The One who Himself is the Word, the One whom God had promised, came to participate in our world as a Man. He created all things and has been steering the course of the history of mankind. God has always been involved in the history of man and still is today. He has also participated in this history in person in the body of a man. He came into the world even though, when He came to His own, those who were His own did not receive Him.

2

From Life to Eternal Life

John 1:4-5

The God who appears in Genesis had the ability to see.
He was the Creator of the heaven and the earth.
He gave commands, and He reveals His actions.
Since God is the One who carried out all things,
He cannot be compared with any of the gods that man has made.

John 1:4-5

[4]In him was life; and the life was the light of men.

[5]And the light shineth in darkness; and the darkness comprehended it not.

We Have Seen That Eternal Life

"In him was life; and the life was the light of men." John 1:4

"In him"–that is, in the Word, in God, in the Creator–there was life. Also, the life of God shone through all the things that He made. Nothing came into being without this life. In the same way, the Word of life was given to man from the very beginning.

"[A]nd the life was the light of men."

What sort of life becomes the light of men? Let's take a look at what the apostle John wrote about this "life."

"That which was from the beginning, which we have heard, which we have seen with our eyes, which we have looked upon, and our hands have handled, of the Word of life; (For the life was manifested, and we have seen it, and bear witness, and shew unto you that eternal life, which was with the Father, and was manifested unto us)." 1 John 1:1-2

Who is this talking about? It is Jesus, isn't it? It is not anyone else. The apostles saw Jesus with their own eyes, touched Him with their own hands, and conversed with Him face to face as they spent time with Him. So they could say that they had seen this eternal life.

"That which was from the beginning . . . the Word of life." 1 John 1:1

"That which was from the beginning, which we have heard." From whom had the apostles heard about the Word of life that was from the beginning? They had heard directly from Jesus. Let's take a look in the Bible at one such scene in progress. One day, Jesus went up on a mountain side and a large crowd gathered around Him.

"And seeing the multitudes, he went up into a mountain: and when he was set, his disciples came unto him: And he opened his mouth, and taught them, saying, Blessed are the poor in spirit: for theirs is the kingdom of heaven." Matthew 5:1-3

Wasn't this how they saw Jesus with their own eyes and heard His words with their own ears? They heard the words of the Son of God.

One day, one of the disciples said to Jesus:

"Lord, shew us the Father." John 14:8

Jesus replied:

"[H]e that hath seen me hath seen the Father." John 14:9

Even though Jesus had come into this world as God, people failed to recognize Him.

Something like this happens occasionally, doesn't it? Suppose you were asked to go to the airport and pick up someone you had never seen before. You are told beforehand the time of the person's arrival, the color of his clothes, the details of his hairstyle, and maybe you are even given a description of his suitcase. You arrive at the gate at the appointed time but find no one there who fits the description you have been given. Later, you find out that the man had been there, but you had not recognized him because he had been wearing an extra coat against the sudden cold. That extra garment will have prevented you from recognizing him.

In much the same way, Jesus came into this world according to all the prophecies and promises recorded in the Old Testament, but people did not recognize Jesus because He came to the world not only as a Man, but in the form of a bondservant.

Nevertheless, there was someone who met Him, recognized Him, and told others about Him, and that someone was the apostle John.

John wrote that Jesus was with the Father but came into this world as a Man. He also said that Jesus was eternal life. How have we regarded this God until now? Have we perhaps been worshipping some false image, mistaking it for God?

An Altar to the Unknown God

Let's consider the case of the Athenians. When the apostle Paul visited Athens (a Greek city filled with talk of all kinds of mythical gods), he observed that the Athenians had built various temples, statues, and altars to worship gods. As Paul addressed these people who did not know the true God, he cried out, saying:

> "Men of Athens, I perceive that in all things ye are too superstitious. For as I passed by, and beheld your devotions, I found an altar with this inscription, TO THE UNKNOWN GOD. Whom therefore ye ignorantly worship, him declare I unto you. God that made the world and all things therein, seeing that he is Lord of heaven and earth, dwelleth not in temples made with hands." Acts 17:22-24

Paul said that the God who created the universe and everything in it is the Creator of the heaven and the earth. As the first verse of Genesis says, "In the beginning God created the heaven and the earth" Genesis 1:1. Taking this first verse of Genesis as a yardstick, let's take a look at how people around the world have thought of God until now.

Over the centuries, people have come up with countless religions. Even today, new religions still appear all the time, and this trend will probably continue until the last day of human history. Even in the days when the Bible was being recorded, people were making and worshipping idols in all shapes and sizes. The God who appears in the first chapter of Genesis, however, bears no shape or form that can be said to have been crafted.

Throughout the world, there are many idols and other objects of worship that people have made and before which they bow down. In Thailand, for example, there is a statue of a reclining Buddha as large as a house. Despite its well-built physique, it does not move an inch. Even when the statue was near completion and the stone carvers were working away at the thinner parts of its ears, the statue itself was completely unaware of what was happening. It has neither nerves nor feelings; there is no life in it, so even if someone were to harm it, it would not be capable of bristling with anger or rebuking the offender.

On the other hand, what about the Bible? The Bible was written in the most captivating of styles during days in which philosophers, scientists, and historians were researching and examining the many and various events that had occurred in human history and the would-be conquerors of this world were engaged in all kinds of battles with each other. What kind of God appears in this Bible that was written in the midst of such circumstances? Since we have drawn close to God's word, we know that God is truly great, but let's take a closer look at what God is really like.

The God who appears in Genesis chapter 1 had the ability to see, He created this world, and He gave commands. This is the image of God that is presented to us. Also, the Creator of the heaven and the earth allows His actions to be seen by man. No idol or other object of worship has such abilities. If you laid out some food before a statue, you would not hear it suddenly demanding more. There is not an idol on earth that can think for itself or act on its own initiative.

In the Beginning God Created the Heaven and the Earth

By virtue of His accomplishments, the God referred to in the verse that says, "In the beginning God created the heaven and the earth" Genesis 1:1, is a magnificent Being far beyond comparison with any idol or object of worship. Can this God be compared to any man-made deity? There is simply no comparison. These man-made idols are completely lifeless. Man may do everything in his power to make his own god, his own religion, and his own objects of worship, but idols carved and shaped to please men's eyes are lifeless and cannot possibly generate any thoughts, give any commands, or carry out any actions of their own.

A computer specialist once said to me:

"In the future, computers will become so advanced that they will be able to outwit man even when it comes to complicated games like chess."

Matters can always backfire on us. A man may go out to hunt a deer and end up accidentally shooting and killing himself. A person may produce a robot that looks like a man and it may be installed with a computer to make it act like a man, but it will never be able to give its own commands or come up with its own creations.

No matter how sophisticated computers may become, all of their actions will still have to be controlled and directed by their programmer. Computers can calculate much faster than the human brain, but they are still man-made objects. Man may create a computer that resembles a human being, but he cannot give life to it. A lifeless object cannot produce life; only life can produce life. It is because man is able to reproduce that we ourselves have been born into the world. We have life within us when we are born into this world, and we are thus able to pass it on to the next generation. Since life itself is hidden away inside us, we cannot see it, but we all have life.

"In the beginning God created the heaven and the earth. And the earth was without form, and void; and darkness was upon the face of the deep. And the Spirit of God moved upon the face of the waters. And God said, Let there be light: and there was light."

Genesis 1:1-3

God said, "Let there be light." This is different from what happens when people turn on a lamp or something similar. Even as God said, "Let there be light," the light was there. This is because God is the very essence of light.

"And God saw the light, that it was good." Genesis 1:4

People have made all kinds of idols for themselves. They set offerings of food before these idols, but the statues cannot smile or enjoy the offerings. They cannot smell the food put in front of them. They do not have the ability to see or know anything. Such inanimate objects have been worshipped for thousands of years and many of them have crumbled into dust. No one can depend on any objects of worship they have made with their own hands. Even if a person worships such an idol his whole life long, that idol will never be able to know him or do anything at all for him. There is a world of difference between knowing and not knowing.

God knew the nature of darkness and so He said, "Let there be light." If there is a sudden power outage at night, don't we wish that the lights would come back on? God, too, was not pleased with the darkness and so He commanded that there be light.

> "And God said, Let there be light: and there was light. And God saw the light, that it was good."

Wouldn't we feel frustrated if we could not distinguish between good and bad, bitter and sweet? Sometimes we may describe a person as being completely ignorant, but there is no one more ignorant than these man-made objects of worship that know absolutely nothing at all. God knows everything in the heavens and on the earth, and He alone. Also, God was able to make divisions.

36

"And God saw the light, that it was good: and God divided the light from the darkness. God called the light Day, and the darkness he called Night. And the evening and the morning were the first day."

Genesis 1:4-5

God divided the day from the night, the light from the darkness. He was able to make this division and He did. We may think lightly of the verse that says, "In the beginning God created the heaven and the earth" Genesis 1:1, taking this for granted since God is all-powerful, but that is not the way we should look at this matter. If we consider these words carefully, we can see life stirring within them; we can see the fountainhead of life.

"And God said, Let there be a firmament in the midst of the waters, and let it divide the waters from the waters. And God made the firmament, and divided the waters which were under the firmament from the waters which were above the firmament: and it was so."

Genesis 1:6-7

God made commands and brought about divisions. He manifested power, the power of life in its entirety. It is in this God, and no other, that we believe.

For Such a Worm as I

Coming to know this God and receiving salvation and eternal life through the Bible is no ordinary matter. Man simply lives his life attached to this tiny planet called Earth.

When I was a child, we used outhouses. If you looked down between the boards of the outhouse, you would see swarms of maggots wiggling around. When the excrement was thrown out on to the field as fertilizer, these maggots would die as they dried up in the sun. As I observed this during my youth I thought:

"Our lives are just the same; we live and die just like that!"

Then I would feel really heavyhearted. Do we have any reason to boast as we live our lives in this way? We all have equally pitiful lives. When I consider this fact, I can readily identify with the hymn that includes the verse:

> Alas! and did my Savior bleed,
> And did my Sovereign die?
> Would He devote that sacred head
> For such a worm as I?[1]

Once we die and are laid in the ground, our bodies decay, and worms creep in and out of our eyes and mouths. This happens to all of us. What pitiful creatures we are!

Think about it. What do we have to show for ourselves? We all die in one way or another. Death is unavoidable, whether we commit suicide by jumping out of a high building, have a heart attack while walking along the street, or are run over and killed by a drunk driver. Is it God's will that we should simply be born and die without aim or reason? Surely, this is a question that is worth considering. The Bible tells us that it was never God's intention for us to die meaninglessly.[2]

Out of Death into Life

We mill around and contend with one another on our tiny planet in the midst of the vast universe full of stars, and yet, God has promised eternal life to each one of us. Do we receive this kind of promise every day? Is eternal life a matter to be taken lightly? The One who came to offer us this priceless and tremendous gift of eternal life has participated in each and every event of human history that has taken place in this world.

In the Bible, there is a verse that says:

"Verily, verily, I say unto you, He that heareth my word, and believeth on him that sent me, hath everlasting life, and shall not come into condemnation, but is passed from death unto life." John 5:24

It may happen that a person will read this verse and find the darkness leaves his heart as he realizes, "My sins have been pardoned! I have been forgiven! I have eternal redemption!" Don't people have that kind of experience? This is because there is life within the words of the Bible and there is light within that life. This is what allows the eyes of our hearts to see, so that we come to realize the truth.

Why does this experience occur in our hearts? Is this an ordinary everyday event? We may make an attempt to describe what has happened to us but simply end up saying that it was good. Perhaps we cannot give this experience adequate expression, but I do not think anyone would be ready to exchange what he has received in this way for anything else that life has to offer. It is an experience that is very real and only comes about because of the power of God, contained within His word. It comes about through God's word and cannot be accomplished by any other power. I feel the greatness of God's love to the core of my being. Had God not bound our lives tightly with His yoke, we would stubbornly live as we please. Perhaps you know this hymn:

> Majestic sweetness sits enthroned
> Upon the Saviour's brow;
> His head with radiant glories crowned,
> His lips with grace o'erflow.
> His lips with grace o'erflow.
>
> No mortal can with Him compare,
> Among the sons of men;
> Fairer is He than all the fair
> Who fill the heav'nly train,
> Who fill the heav'nly train.

> He saw me plunged in deep distress,
> He flew to my relief;
> For me He bore the shameful Cross
> And carried all my grief,
> And carried all my grief.
>
> To Him I owe my life and breath,
> And all the joys I have;
> He makes me triumph over death.
> And saves me from the grave,
> And saves me from the grave.
>
> Since from His bounty I receive,
> Such proofs of love divine,
> Had I a thousand hearts to give,
> Lord, they should all be Thine,
> Lord, they should all be Thine.[3]

When we look back on days gone by, we realize that all our worries and daily affairs are experiences common to everyone in the world. These experiences may differ slightly in nature, but we all live through similar joys and sorrows. In the midst of all these affairs, however, we carry something different within us, don't we? The above hymn puts it in this way:

> To Him I owe my life and breath,
> And all the joys I have.

This life does not just appear out of nowhere; it is given through God's word.

> "Being born again, not of corruptible seed, but of incorruptible, by the word of God, which liveth and abideth for ever."   1 Peter 1:23

Can anything in the world compare to the fact that there is life within God's word? Everything of which this world can boast, all put together, cannot compare to God's holy word.

Help Me!

What does man come to this world to find? Can we find fulfillment, for example, in bringing children into the world? Children give us just as many worries as they do joys. There is even a Korean proverb that says, "Happy is the lot of those who remain childless." It is also a mistake to think that a wealthy person is free from concern. Indeed, the more money a person has, the more his worries. Perhaps it would be better to be born and live as a fool, since a fool does not seem to have any worries. He will wear a smile on his face even if he has no money at all or walks around undressed in freezing weather. On the other hand, when it comes to knowledge, even just a little of it can cause quite a headache.

We are born into this world and as we are growing up we learn to read and then gradually we use this skill to build up our store of knowledge. It is truly remarkable that in the process of all this, we can come to realize, through the Bible, something that is greater than anything else in this world.

These days, if you do not know anything about computers and the Internet, you might be described as computer- or Internet-illiterate. It is helpful to have a little knowledge about such things, but there is something much more important that we ought to know.

There is a story about a genteel scholar who was on board a small ferryboat. A brawny young ferryman stood at the back steering the boat across the river, as the scholar sat fanning himself, wondering if the ferryman had ever learned to read and write.

"Young man!" he said. "Have you studied any of the classics?"

"I've never been to school, let alone studied the classics. I just earn my living rowing this boat."

"What! A man must study something. You have to learn to read and write. Aren't you ashamed of being illiterate, young man?"

"You think I should study? I don't have time for that kind of thing. I'm too busy trying to earn a living. I have to go back and forth across this river all day long."

This pedantic scholar had turned up out of the blue and done nothing but scold and belittle the ferryman. Then suddenly, a crack of thunder sounded in the sky, it began to rain hard, and the waves began to beat against the boat, rocking it violently. The scholar held on to his hat and became paralyzed with fear. Then the ferryman asked him, "Do you know how to swim, sir?"

"No, I've never learned."

"At times like this, sir, you don't need to know the classics, and neither do you need a university education; if you can't swim, you die."

"Oh my goodness!" the scholar cried out. "You've got to help me. Please don't let the boat sink!"

What is more precious than life?

We all live in different ways, but life itself is precious to all of us. Yet is there anything at all in life that we can be truly confident about? Everything in this world perishes and crumbles eventually. That includes us too, doesn't it? We, too, are like leaves that fall to the ground. If we look at the fallen leaves in autumn, we can see veins spread out like a spider's web in each leaf. In midsummer, water flows into those veins, keeping the leaves green and healthy so that when the wind blows, they do not fall. By autumn, however, the veins that have supplied water and nourished the green leaves throughout the summer are mere traces of life. Our lives also wither away just like these autumn leaves.

You Must Go, and So Must I

When I was a child, there was a song that the girls in particular used to sing as they played. None of the boys could play the game but the girls would gather their skirts together and hop up and down around a stretched-out band of elastic. These girls were as light and nimble as butterflies, but the song they sang was very sad. The girls holding the elastic would sing, "Autumn leaf, tumbling in the wind, where are you going?"

Then the girls jumping would answer, "This naked body is cold, so terribly cold."

They were such mournful words and yet the girls would play on, completely oblivious to the depressing lyrics of their song.

I was often ill as a child and, as a result, I became well aware of just how much man's life is like a leaf that falls in the autumn. Whenever I was ill, I would lie down on my mattress and think to myself:

"After I die, trains will still be heard as they come and go. When I am dead and buried, there will still be the sound of children playing outside."

Even when I was young I was aware that life must end like the leaves in autumn. I knew that human life comes to an end. Before I came to know the gospel, when evening came I would sit by the windowsill and sing a melancholy song.

> Ah! You must go, and so must I.
> Just as the night comes when the day is over,
> The sun also sets on our love.

This was before I even knew what love was. I would just sing away.

> The snow is forming drifts in the country village on a winter's evening, A candle burns brightly and I cry alone.

As the wind howled outside, my heart would melt away like a dying candle.

"Ah! Some day you will die, and I will die too."

I would think of my friends who had already left me and gone away, and I would feel a deep melancholy.

What a tremendous blessing I have received since then! Words simply cannot express it. Were it not for the gospel, I would now be feeling infinitely lonely, and all the more so with each passing day and each glance in the mirror.

These days, as I brush my teeth, I look in the mirror and sometimes think to myself:

"You've really changed a lot, haven't you? You'd like to live for another hundred years, wouldn't you? But take a good look at your teeth. Do you think you'll be able to use them even for twenty or thirty more years? They're already getting worn and loose."

I'm already growing old. Aging and decay pursue us like the wind. Our bodies wear out like ragged clothes, but we continually deceive ourselves with illusions of youth. If a tooth falls out, a dentist can replace it with a false tooth so we are not even aware ourselves of how much we are changing. We put a bit of color in our graying hair and are pleased with our more youthful appearance, even though we are actually continuing to age. In certain respects, man is really a melancholy being. Wouldn't you agree?

To Him I Owe my Life and Breath

The One whom we are to serve, is not in front of us, nor is He behind or next to us. The hymn I referred to earlier contains the line:

> To Him I owe my life and breath.

He is the very life within us, but when does this begin? It begins on the day we realize the truth of the gospel. On the day of this new beginning, the word of life enters us and holds the power of life within us. What would have happened if the God in whom we believe had not been the God who said, "Let there be light" and "saw the light, that it was good"? It is the power of the One who spoke in this way that enables us to see His light through the Bible and come to realize that it is good. That power abides within us. The object of our worship is not something that belongs to others. It does not lie somewhere up in the heavens; it is inside us. He dwells within us, within all those whose sins have been pardoned. The object of worship for all those who have come to know the love of Christ is not to be found up there in the skies; He abides within us.

He may seem obscured by the petty events and problems of our daily lives, but He dwells within us from the day we realize the truth of the gospel. We need to be aware that this holy work has been accomplished within us and live our lives accordingly.

> "For the hope which is laid up for you in heaven, whereof ye heard before in the word of the truth of the gospel; Which is come unto you, as it is in all the world; and bringeth forth fruit, as it doth in you, since the day ye heard of it, and knew the grace of God in truth."
>
> Colossians 1:5-6

It says here, "the day ye heard of it, and knew the grace of God in truth."

> O happy bond that seals my vows.
> To Him who merits all my love:
> Let cheerful anthems fill His house,
> While to that sacred shrine I move.
>
> Happy day, happy day,
> When Jesus washed my sins away.
> He taught me how to watch and pray,
> And live rejoicing every day.
> Happy day, happy day,
> When Jesus washed my sins away.[4]

Does this hymn express something that everyone has experienced? The word of promise given to us through the Bible is accomplished within us. The words of truth are planted within us. Whether you come to realize God's grace while singing a hymn, while reading the Bible, or while listening to a sermon, the important point is that you have come to know God's love.

And the Life Was the Light of Men

> "In him was life; and the life was the light of men."   John 1:4

This verse tells us that there was life in the Word that existed from the beginning, and that this life was the light of men. Light may be emitted from various sources. It may shine from an electric lamp, illuminating the objects in its range, and it may project an image into cameras and onto screens.

The light referred to in this verse, however, does not shine on inanimate objects or creatures such as birds and animals; it is "the light of men."

> Eager eyes are watching, longing,
> For the lights along the shore.[5]

People become frustrated, distressed, and lonely because they are unable to find this light for which they long. At such times, they try to throw their hearts and minds into some activity or another, but their efforts again turn out to be in vain. Whether in education, in money-making, or in some other aspect of their lives, people try very hard to discover a true light, but none of these endeavors can bring absolute fulfillment to man. Nothing in the society of man is able to do this.

What sort of light is the Bible referring to when it says, "the life was the light of men"? In one of the Psalms it says:

"Thy word is a lamp unto my feet, and a light unto my path."
Psalm 119:105

Before the advent of street lamps, people always carried lanterns with them whenever they went out after dark. In a similar way, the word of God lights up the path that lies ahead of us as we journey through life. "Thy word is a lamp unto my feet, and a light unto my path." Christians need to experience fully the significance of these words in their daily lives.

"In him was life, and the life was the light of men." John 1:4

"In him was life." In God was life. Then when it says here that "the life was the light of men," it is telling us that this life is passed on to us and through it we are able to meet God. That is when our fate is determined. The true light appeared to men and thus "the life was the light of men."

Animals and vegetation also need light to grow and live, and the light shines on the fields that form their habitat. Such physical light, however, is merely a shadow of the true eternal light of God. Sunlight is really dazzling. If you stand with your back to the sun and spray water into the sunlight, you can see a miniature rainbow, a radiant image of light.

Light contains many invisible rays, such as infrared and ultra-violet rays. It also provides essential nourishment and energy for all physical life. Vegetation receives energy from the sunlight. If we do not receive enough sunlight as we grow, we may develop a vitamin D deficiency. Just as sunlight is vital for plants and animals, God's word is the light that has given life to man from the beginning. All things came into being by God's word.

> "But if our gospel be hid, it is hid to them that are lost: In whom the god of this world hath blinded the minds of them which believe not, lest the light of the glorious gospel of Christ, who is the image of God, should shine unto them. For we preach not ourselves, but Christ Jesus the Lord; and ourselves your servants for Jesus' sake. For God, who commanded the light to shine out of darkness, hath shined in our hearts, to give the light of the knowledge of the glory of God in the face of Jesus Christ." 2 Corinthians 4:3-6

The God "who commanded the light to shine out of darkness" has shone into our hearts the light that is in the face of Jesus Christ. On the day that this light shone into our hearts, we did not actually see Jesus in person, but our hearts were brightened. It is precisely this light that gives life to men. If this light of the gospel is veiled, it is veiled to those who are perishing. This is why it is necessary for us to consider the message of the Bible once more.

And the Light Shineth in Darkness; and the Darkness Comprehended It Not

> "And the light shineth in darkness; and the darkness comprehended it not." John 1:5

The light shone in darkness, but the darkness did not comprehend it. The darkness here does not refer to darkness in general, but to the darkness in people's hearts. One day, Satan's words entered into man's heart as he said, "For God doth know that in the day ye eat thereof [of the fruit of the tree of knowledge of good and evil], then your eyes shall be opened" Genesis 3:5. When man ate this fruit, his eyes, once clear, became full of greed and real darkness.

Man turned his back on God and his eyes became dim, so God has continually proclaimed His Word to man in order that man's darkened eyes might see clearly once more. In eating the forbidden fruit, man disobeyed God's first command. God had said that the man was not to eat this fruit. Nevertheless, God took pity upon man the transgressor and all his descendants, and in order to give His Word to man, He chose a nation of people amongst whom He sent the Christ. The verse, "the light shineth in darkness; and the darkness comprehended it not," expresses the fact that man's darkened heart did not accept God's Word.

I once read an account of a young Chinese noblewoman who had come to realize the truth of the gospel. She compared this moment of realization to what happens when a large flower pot is lifted up. All the insects that live in the dark and damp underneath the pot scatter as soon as they are exposed to the light. She said that this was how free and easy her heart had become. Our hearts, too, crawl with all kinds of thoughts and feelings, but the day comes when we are able to sing:

> I have light in my soul for which long I have sought,
> Since Jesus came into my heart.[6]

When the light shines into our hearts, all the darkness there quietly disappears. The words "the darkness comprehended it not" no longer apply to those who have received the true light. When the apostle John wrote, "the darkness comprehended it not," he was referring to those who were in the darkness and did not receive the Light, even though this Light had come to them.

3

The Light of Lights

John 1:6-18

The lights on this earth are a shadow of the true light.
"God, who commanded the light to shine out of darkness" has shone
into our hearts the light that is in the face of Jesus Christ.
This is the light that gives life to man.
We are the vessels that are to be filled with this light.

John 1:6-18

⁶There was a man sent from God, whose name was John. ⁷The same came for a witness, to bear witness of the Light, that all men through him might believe. ⁸He was not that Light, but was sent to bear witness of that Light.

⁹That was the true Light, which lighteth every man that cometh into the world. ¹⁰He was in the world, and the world was made by him, and the world knew him not. ¹¹He came unto his own, and his own received him not. ¹²But as many as received him, to them gave the power to become the sons of God, even to them that believe on his name: ¹³which were born, not of blood, nor of the will of the flesh, nor of the will of man, but of God.

¹⁴And the Word was made flesh, and dwelt among us, (and we beheld his glory, the glory as of the only begotten of the Father,) full of grace and truth.

¹⁵John bare witness of him and cried, saying, this was he of whom I spake, He that cometh after me is preferred before me: for he was before me.

¹⁶And of his fulness have all we received, and grace for grace. ¹⁷For the law was given by Moses, but grace and truth came by Jesus Christ. ¹⁸No man hath seen God at any time; the only begotten Son, which is in the bosom of the Father, he hath declared him.

The True Light, Which Lighteth Every Man

"There was a man sent from God, whose name was John."   John 1:6

The John who appears here is not the apostle John who wrote John's Gospel; it is the prophet John who came baptizing. John the Baptist was a prophet who came to bear witness of Jesus, the Christ.

"The same came for a witness, to bear witness of the Light, that all men through him might believe."   John 1:7

When it says that he came to "bear witness of the light," it means that he came to bear witness of Jesus. Who is Jesus? He is God who came to this world having first spoken through the prophets in Old Testament times. John the Baptist bore witness of this God, the Word.

"He was not that Light, but was sent to bear witness of that Light."
John 1:8

John the Baptist himself was not the true light; he simply came to this world in order to indicate the One who was the true light.

"That was the true Light which lighteth every man that cometh into the world."   John 1:9

How many times does "light" appear in this passage up to verse 9? Let's read through again from verse 4 and see.

"In him was life; and the life was the light of men. And the light shineth in darkness; and the darkness comprehended it not. There was a man sent from God, whose name was John. The same came for a witness, to bear witness of the Light, that all men through him might believe. He was not that Light, but was sent to bear witness of that Light. That was the true Light, which lighteth every man that cometh into the world."   John 1:4-9

How many times is it? Seven times. This is a matter of deep significance. In the Bible, the number seven is the perfect number of God.

One day as Jesus was preaching in the temple, He said, "I am the light of the world." As He said this, the seven lamps of the candlestick were burning in the temple.

> "Then spake Jesus again unto them, saying, I am the light of the world: he that followeth me shall not walk in darkness, but shall have the light of life."
>
> John 8:12

Jesus is the light of the world.

Some years ago, while traveling overseas, I drove through a village and noticed a candlestick with seven branches carved onto the main doors of one of the buildings. There was one main stem in the middle with three branches on each side. Such a candlestick placed in front of a building or carved on the walls generally indicates a Jewish synagogue. The candlestick appears in the Old Testament in the book of Exodus and again in the New Testament in the book of Revelation.

A candlestick was intended to provide light. The candlestick in the Old Testament was not made according to the whims of the craftsmen; it was formed according to the specific design that God gave to Moses. The candlestick was made from a large piece of gold and weighed about 34 kilograms (75 lbs.), so it must have been very big. It took about one talent[1] of pure gold to make the candlestick, its tongs, the snuffdishes, and the other vessels for the temple.

Thou Shalt Make a Candlestick of Pure Gold

The candlestick was not easily crafted. It was not that a smith melted down some metal, poured it into a mold, and waited for it to set. It was hammered into shape out of one piece of pure gold. Even the intricate shapes of the almonds were to be hammered out. Only then would the candlestick be made in accordance with God's instructions. Exodus chapter 25 verses 31 to 40 contain the detailed instructions regarding this process that God gave to Moses on Mount Sinai.

> "And thou shalt make a candlestick of pure gold: of beaten work shall the candlestick be made: his shaft, and his branches, his bowls, his knops, and his flowers shall be of the same. And six branches shall come out of the sides of it; three branches of the candlestick out of the one side, and three branches of the candlestick out of the other side: three bowls made like unto almonds, with a knop and a flower in one branch; and three bowls made like almonds in the other branch, with a knop and a flower: so in the six branches that come out of the candlestick. And in the candlestick shall be four bowls made like unto almonds, with their knops and their flowers. And there shall be a knop under two branches of the same, and a knop under two branches of the same, and a knop under two branches of the same, according to the six branches that proceed out of the candlestick." Exodus 25:31-35

The phrase "of the same" indicates clearly that all the parts of the candlestick were connected and they were all fashioned from one single piece of gold.

> "Their knops and their branches shall be of one same: all of it shall be one beaten work of pure gold. And thou shalt make the seven lamps thereof: and they shall light the lamps thereof, that they give light over against it. And the tongs thereof, and the snuffdishes thereof, shall be of pure gold. Of a talent of pure gold shall he make it, with all these vessels. And look that thou you make them after their pattern which was shewed thee in the mount." Exodus 25:36-40

According to this passage, the candlestick had three branches extending from each side of its central stem. There were seven lamps altogether; one at the top of the stem and one at the end of each branch. God instructed the Israelites to make this candlestick, not by melting down the gold and pouring it into a mold, but by hammering out its shape.

The extent to which God gave all the detailed instructions is amazing.

"Three bowls made like unto almonds, with a knop and a flower in one branch."

These instructions were very specific. The knops here were like saucers under the flowers. The craftsmen would have had a hard time hammering out all these bowls, knops, and flowers to follow to the letter the directions that the aging Moses had received from God. The delicate knobs and flowers were also to be hammered out along with the candlestick itself. God said that it was all to be hammered out.

This passage seems to suggest that God trains us through hardships, hammering us down into His candlestick. The magnificent knops of the lamps were all hammered into shape in order that each of the lamps could be erected. Similarly, God's hammerings of trials and tribulations will continue to sound until the day we go before Him. Until that day, we must constantly struggle with hardships as we live in this world.

Jesus said, "I am the light of the world" John 8:12; 9:5. He also said, "Ye are the light of the world" Matthew 5:14. As believers, we have to go through hardships in order that the light of Jesus might be revealed to the world through us. We need to understand that since Jesus suffered, we too must participate in His suffering. We can always choose to avoid hardships and live an easy life, but we have now seen how the candlestick was made according to specific instructions and for a specific purpose. We are vessels that are to be filled with Jesus Christ, who is the Light. So it is our responsibility to allow ourselves to be hammered down and subjected to constant training until we stand before Him.

To the Seven Churches

As we saw earlier, "light" appears seven times in the passage in John chapter 1 verses 4 through 9. This was how the apostle John bore witness to Jesus, and it is this light that illuminates the seven churches.

> "John, to the seven churches which are in Asia: ... Saying, I am Alpha and Omega, the first and the last: and, What thou seest, write in a book, and send it unto the seven churches which are in Asia; unto Ephesus, and unto Smyrna, to Pergamos, and unto Thyatira, and unto Sardis, and unto Philadelphia, and unto Laodicea."
>
> Revelation 1:4, 11

Here we have reference to seven churches. The Book of Revelation goes on to tell us that the seven candlesticks are the seven churches.

> "Write the things which thou hast seen, and the things which are, and the things which shall be hereafter; the mystery of the seven stars which thou sawest in my right hand, and the seven golden candlesticks. The seven stars are the angels of the seven churches: and the seven candlesticks which thou sawest are the seven churches."
>
> Revelation 1:19-20

When it says here, "the things which shall be hereafter," it is not referring to the future from our present point in time; it is a reference to the future from the point in time of the apostle John.

Revelation chapters 2 and 3 describe in detail the different characteristics of each of the seven churches. The history of Christianity has passed through seven distinct stages that correspond to these seven churches, and each of these churches has its own unique characteristic. We can see how the believers in each age have been through sufferings and hardships.

The believers in the first of these churches, the church of Ephesus, went through many ordeals. They drove out any false teachers and carefully differentiated between those who were true believers and those who were not. Nevertheless, the Bible tells us that they were rebuked on one account. It says that they left their first love.

The second of these churches, the church of Smyrna, also went through a particularly harrowing period of ordeal and martyrdom. We too must face this kind of battle in our faith. The Bible provides us with a role model in the believers who have gone before us, having shone the light into the world in this way like the shining candlestick. Through passages like this in the Bible, we can see how this light is shining, and how we should live so that it shines out in some small way through our lives as well.

Out of Thee Shall He Come Forth unto Me that Is to Be Ruler in Israel

> "That was the true Light, which lighteth every man that cometh into the world. He was in the world, and the world was made by him, and the world knew him not." John 1:9-10

It says here that the light came to this world, but the world did not know Him. In verse 5 it says, "And the light shineth in darkness; and the darkness comprehended it not," but what is the point of emphasis in verse 9? It says, "every man." "Every man" indicates each one of us, doesn't it? Self-examination through God's word is the responsibility of each one of us individually. Faith is our personal responsibility, as the light shines on each of us as individuals.

> "He came to his own, and his own did not received him not."
>
> John 1:11

In the midst of the vast universe with its billions of stars, God created the tiny planet of Earth and there He planted a garden - the Garden of Eden. Then He created man and placed him in the garden. As a result of this first man's disobedience, God drove him from the garden. Generations later, God commanded Abraham to leave Ur of the Chaldees for a land far away that God would show him. God led him to the land of Canaan, the location of present-day Israel. There Abraham and his family settled, and there his descendants established a nation. It was to this land, and to this nation, that Jesus came.

The birth of Jesus was like that of no other person. Even before He came, the prophecies regarding the process by which He would come into the world and the events that would surround His birth had all been recorded in great detail. The prophets had looked far into the future and even revealed the name of the little town in the land of Israel in which Jesus would be born.

> "But thou, Bethlehem Ephratah, though thou be little among the thousands of Judah, yet out of you shall come forth unto me that is to be ruler in Israel; whose goings forth have been from of old, from everlasting."
>
> Micah 5:2

As indicated in this verse, the birthplace of Jesus was Bethlehem. He came in accordance with the written word of God, according to the seed of the word that had been received and proclaimed by the prophets, who used expressions such as, "Thus the Lord said to me" and, "The word of the Lord also came to me saying" to indicate that

God was speaking through them. Jesus was born in the flesh in the very land that God had indicated through His prophets.

Here in verse 9 it talks about "the true Light, which lighteth every man." This Light is the One who came as the true Light. When Jesus came to the land of Israel, however, the Jews did not receive Him. They did not recognize Him. Just as they rejected the One who was born in their land, we tend to be lacking in faith even though we appear to receive God's word into our hearts.

As individuals, we have nothing of which to boast. We are self-centered and egotistical, but the day comes when God's word quietly descends upon our hearts, and we come to believe. Then we are able to sing the hymn that says:

> The love of God is greater far
> Than tongue or pen can ever tell.[2]

When this inexpressible power takes hold of our hearts, we come to think once again about Jesus and His aim in coming into this world. Not even an orchestra comprising all the instruments in this world would suffice to praise God adequately for His birth.

For I Could Wish that Myself Were Accursed from Christ

It is worth taking a moment here to consider some of the words that Paul wrote about two thousand years ago, words that reveal an attitude that is difficult for us to imagine with our limited minds and narrow viewpoint.

> "I say the truth in Christ, I lie not, my conscience also bearing me witness in the Holy Ghost, that I have great heaviness and continual sorrow in my heart. For I could wish that myself were accursed from Christ for my brethren, my kinsmen according to the flesh: who are Israelites; to whom pertaineth the adoption, and the glory, and the

covenants, and the giving of the law, and the service of God, and the promises; whose are the fathers, and of whom as concerning the flesh Christ came, who is over all, God blessed for ever. Amen."

Romans 9:1-5

What was going on in the apostle Paul's heart to lead him to write like this? As I read through the book of Romans, I sometimes wonder whether people really understand Paul's state of mind at this time.

Paul was writing in all earnestness as he expressed the frustrations seething inside him. His heart was full of love for his fellow Jews, and he laid his soul bare as he deeply lamented that God had forsaken his people because they had rejected His love, His plan, and all that He had promised them.

The apostle John wrote of the Jews' rejection of Jesus in a gentle and simple manner: "He came unto his own, and his own received him not" John 1:11, but Paul did not speak in such a way; his words reveal his distress. Here in Romans chapter 9, Paul wrote, "I say the truth in Christ." Let's consider for a moment the ardent sincerity of Paul's heart at that time.

As Paul thought about his fellow countrymen, he expressed frankly the deep and endless anguish in his heart. Paul's fellow countrymen had been rejected and he expressed his deep distress regarding this matter as he said that he was ready even to be cast into hell if it would mean that his fellow countrymen would receive God's love and be saved.

According to the flesh, Christ was born to the Israelites, but what kind of Person was Jesus? This Man was Christ, "who is over all, God blessed for ever." This God was ostracized by His own people, so Paul was expressing how much he pitied the Jews, his own flesh and blood, for their act of betrayal.

> "Brethren, my heart's desire and prayer to God for Israel is, that they might be saved."
>
> Romans 10:1

Such was the heart's desire of Paul. He had a tremendous love for his people, a love that was different from the kind of patriotism of ordinary people who have a real love for their country and their fellow countrymen. This love was also different from that of a politician with his own interests at heart. Every country has its poets and writers who have expressed their endless love for their people and sacrificed their lives for their fellow countrymen.

As Paul continued to teach the Bible and spread the gospel to people of other nations, his love for his own people cried out from the depths of his heart.

As we have seen, Jesus came to the land of Israel and to the Jews, who had received the promise and been waiting for Him to come and bring them the word of God, but they rejected Him. As a result, the gospel began to spread outside of Israel. It is by virtue of this fact that we too, as Gentiles, have been saved. As Gentiles, we have been able to come to faith in Jesus because, "He came to his own and his own received him not."

By analogy, we might consider the example of an upset child. His mother prepares some delicious food and calls him to come and eat; but because the child is upset, he says, "No, I don't want to!" and turns away. What will the mother do then? She will give the food to one of the other children in the family, and the first child will think, "Why did I have to go and say that?"

Similarly, the Israelites had received the promise and everything had been prepared for them, but who would have known that they would reject the Christ so rashly? As a scholar of the law and a teacher of Israel, Paul was aware of what the Jews had done. This is why he asked us not to take lightly the gift of the gospel that we have received as Gentiles. Such is the deep significance of the words recorded in the New Testament.

His Own Received Him Not

Let's consider the situation at that time that prevented the Jews from receiving Jesus as the Christ. For a long time, the prophets of the Jews had pointed towards the Christ and foretold of His coming, and the Jews themselves were waiting for Him. Before Jesus came to this world, His life from birth to death was prophesied in many passages in the Old Testament. The Scriptures described in detail the way in which He would come to this earth and the way in which He would die. This was all long before Jesus appeared on this earth in the body of a man.

When Jesus was actually born, however, the many priests and scholars of the Scriptures who had been waiting for the coming of the Christ were not able to recognize Him. This is because they thought that when the Christ was born, He would come with tremendous power and influence. The Jews had been attacked so often by foreign powers and had suffered so much under those powers that they longed continually for the restoration of their country, so it was inevitable that they should have such expectations. As a result, they were anticipating a Christ who would come and bring this about for them. The pride of being God's chosen people fueled their desire all the more for a great and powerful Savior.

Thus, despite all the many prophecies regarding Jesus–that is, the Christ–in the Old Testament, when He was actually born, the Jews could neither recognize nor believe that Jesus was the Christ. In their eyes, this Man called Jesus was shabby beyond belief and hardly worth a second glance. They considered Jesus as being far from the Christ that they had imagined. "Christ" means "the anointed One," in other words, "the chosen One of God." They had been waiting for this Savior that God would send into the world, and He actually came to their land, but when they saw Jesus they could not imagine this Man to be the Christ. He was quite different from the person they had had in mind.

After Jesus had departed from this world, the apostles preached Jesus Christ to the Jews who had come to Jerusalem to observe their various feasts: from Ethiopia and Egypt to the south, from Babylonia far away to the east, from Syria to the north, and from various other regions of Asia Minor. The apostles stayed there for several months and kept themselves busy preaching that Jesus was the Christ.

> "And daily in the temple, and in every house, they ceased not to teach and preach Jesus Christ."
>
> Acts 5:42

Since the apostles knew and had come to believe the significance of Jesus' suffering and terrible death, they devoted themselves to spreading the message that He was the Christ.

"Jesus is the Christ!"

These days even if you were to ask people who do not believe in Jesus and never go to church, they would be able to tell you that Jesus was Christ.[3] Everyone knows this. They may not know precisely what this means, but most people are familiar with the name Jesus Christ.

Render to Caesar the Things which Are Caesar's

What was the attitude of the Jews towards Jesus when He was carrying out His ministry on this earth? They felt a deep hostility towards Him. They were very patriotic and zealously sought to protect their beloved Israel. They also had a strong religious zeal. The religious leaders of the Jews often sought to fathom Jesus' intentions by sending their underlings to question Him, or by going and questioning Him directly themselves.

We often come across such incidents in the Gospels of Matthew, Mark, and Luke. The Jews frequently tested Jesus and attempted to force Him into a trap, but Jesus always answered very carefully.

On one occasion the Jews asked Jesus a question regarding the Roman emperor, the enemy of their country. They were hoping to lead Jesus into a trap so that He would be arrested and killed by the Romans. So they asked Jesus whether or not it was right to pay taxes to the Roman emperor.

> "Is it lawful to give tribute unto Caesar, or not?"   Matthew 22:17

Caesar here is Tiberius Caesar, who was the emperor of Rome at the time. The question was a tricky one. If Jesus had declared it unlawful to pay taxes to Caesar, He would have been advocating a violation of the Roman law. On the other hand, if He had said to pay taxes to the Romans, He would have been deemed a traitor of His people, who were under Roman oppression. It was the religious leaders of the Jews[4] who sent their underlings to Jesus to ask this question.

These leaders cursed the tax collectors—people like Zacchaeus—who worked as agents for the Romans, collecting taxes from their own people and handing them over to the oppressors. At that time, even though these tax collectors were their fellow countrymen, the Jews regarded them as being as degenerate as prostitutes and denounced them as treacherous leeches who sucked the very lifeblood out of their own people.

What was it that these religious leaders asked Jesus?

"Is it lawful to give tribute unto Caesar, or not?"

Jesus would have heard of the suffering and struggles that the Jews faced in paying taxes to Rome. Even while Mary was pregnant with Jesus, the Roman emperor–greedy for more efficient collection of taxes–decreed that a census be taken[5] and that everyone under his jurisdiction should register in their home cities.[6]

Similar censuses are still taken from time to time in various countries today. If the greed for more taxes had not driven the emperor Augustus to issue this command, Jesus would not have been born in Bethlehem of Judea in the south, but in Galilee in the north, which was considered a Gentile land. As a result of Caesar's decree far away in the west, Mary, who was nearing the end of her pregnancy, had no choice but to go with her husband to Bethlehem, and so it was that Jesus was born there.

Mary had acted in compliance with the demands of the Roman emperor and now, over thirty years later, when the Jews asked Jesus, "Is it lawful to give tribute unto Caesar, or not?" He neither ordered nor forbade His interrogators to pay taxes to the Romans. His own mother, Mary, had acted in accordance with the command of Caesar, when she went to Bethlehem and there she had given birth to her child, so her Son, Jesus had no reason to oppose such decrees. Still Jesus did not simply tell them they were to pay these taxes. Neither did He tell them to defy the law and refuse to pay. Instead, He said to them:

"Shew me the tribute money" Matthew 22:19, and "bring me a penny, that I may see it" Mark 12:15.

Jesus looked at the inscription on the back of the coin.[7] He was given and asked:

"Whose image and inscription is this?"

They answered, "Caesar's."

So Jesus said, "Render therefore unto Caesar the things which are Caesar's; and unto God the things that are God's."

Jesus' simple and straightforward reply here left his questioners at a loss for words.

"Render therefore unto Caesar the things which are Caesar's."

To Them Gave He Power to Become the Sons of God

> "But as many as received him, to them gave he power to become the sons of God, even to them that believe on his name: which were born, not of blood, nor of the will of the flesh, nor of the will of man, but of God." John 1:12-13

Sons of God are born not of blood, nor of the will of the flesh, but of the will of God. Once we have the right to become sons of God, once we know that these words have shone into our hearts as the true light, we may come up against all kinds of concerns in our lives. Nevertheless, in the midst of all these difficulties, the moment comes when we remember once more that we are sons of God.

> I'm possessed of a hope that is steadfast and sure,
> Since Jesus came into my heart.
> There's a light in the valley of death now for me,

> Since Jesus came into my heart.
> Floods of joy o'er my soul like the sea billows roll,
> Since Jesus came into my heart.[8]

Can money alone solve the problems that arise in our daily lives? Can fame solve such problems? Let's think about it this way. How would you feel if you heard that someone very important was going to visit your home? Would you be indifferent to the news? If it was someone you were really pleased to see, someone for whom you had the deepest respect, you would anticipate that person's coming with joy and excitement. But if Jesus were not just to visit your house, but your heart, how would you feel then?

A young man once told me an amusing story about a time when he had not washed his hands for days. While he was at military training camp, a very distinguished guest had visited the camp. The visitor had chosen to shake hands with him of all the many people there. The young man felt so honored that he wept. Since he had shaken hands with such an honored guest, he did not wash his hands for three days after that. When I asked him what he had done at meal times, he admitted he had eaten with dirty hands. I could see that it is quite possible for a person to behave in such a way. If people react like this to a distinguished person, how would they react if they knew that God, the Creator of the universe, had come to find them?

What can be stronger than the love of the God who came to find us, as it appears here in John chapter 1 verse 12? It says here that to those who received this love, He gave them "power to become the sons of God," and so once we become sons of God in this way, our behavior is all the more important. As we found earlier in the illustration of the seven candles and the seven churches, living as sons of God involves constantly being hammered down into His candlestick throughout our lives. God wishes us to follow Christ's example and live in a manner befitting His children, and it is our responsibility to do this in the course of our lives. How are we living our lives in this world? How are we behaving towards those who do not believe? When we draw near to God's word and it becomes our very own, His light flows out through our lives and is continually passed on.

When we face ordeals or difficulties, we should not necessarily think that God is disciplining us. There are times when God intentionally allows us to undergo trials. We need to go through these experiences. Our lives cannot always be easy.

Behold!

Sometimes I think about the later lives of the people who appear here in John chapter 1. First of all, what about John the Baptist?

> "He [John the Baptist] was not that Light, but was sent to bear witness of that Light."
> John 1:8

John the Baptist was killed as a result of one woman's dance. King Herod was so enchanted by his step-daughter's dancing that he rashly promised to give her anything she wanted, even up to half of his kingdom. The young woman consulted her mother Herodias,[9] who told her to demand that the head of John the Baptist be brought to her on a platter. Thus John was beheaded at the request of this young talented dancer. His death was not even her own personal wish, but that of her mother. John's life came to a pitiful end at the whim of a stranger. Before he died, however, he fulfilled his duty to "bear witness of that Light."

Then there was Peter, who believed in Jesus and later is said to have been crucified upside down. He was a direct eyewitness of the true Light who came into this world.

69

And then what about Jesus Christ, the true Light of whom John the Baptist came to bear witness? He came to this world and at the age of thirty-three, He suffered the wretched death of crucifixion in accordance with the Roman law. But His final words were such that they could not have been uttered by anyone else in the history of mankind: "It is finished." When He said these words and breathed His last, what was it that was finished? His purpose and plan culminated there on the cross; He died only after accomplishing His goal.

Now let's take a look at how these people appeared on the scene and met one another in this world. What did John the Baptist say when he first saw Jesus?

"Behold the Lamb of God, which taketh away the sin of the world."

John 1:29

He said, "Behold." Why did he say this? Didn't they have eyes to see for themselves? These were the words of a man who had the eyes to see something that others could not see, and he had indeed seen it.

"And the Word was made flesh, and dwelt among us, (and we beheld his glory, the glory as of the only begotten of the Father,) full of grace and truth."

John 1:14

The Word was made flesh. All the prophecies that had been made through the prophets long before this culminated in the Christ, as "the Word was made flesh, and dwelt among us."

The disciples saw Jesus with their own eyes. They leaned on Him, they touched Him, and they believed that He was the only begotten Son of God who was in the bosom of the Father. The day came when all the words that God had spoken over a very long period of time through the prophets in the Old Testament gave birth to Jesus. God's word was accomplished down to the smallest detail. The apostles who knew this realized that Jesus was the Son of God and they followed Him. Today, we too come to know through the writings of the apostles that Jesus was the Son of God and we believe in Him.

> Long by the prophets of Israel foretold!
> Gentiles and Jews the blest vision behold.[10]

This blessing is not just given to anyone. It is really something to be proud of when we think that the God who gives this blessing is our God and Savior. This is the foundation of our faith and the Rock on which we stand. One day, Jesus asked His disciples, "Whom do men say that I the Son of man am?"

> "And they said, Some say that thou art John the Baptist: some, Elias; and others, Jeremias, or one of the prophets." Matthew 16:14

Then Jesus asked again, "But whom say ye that I am?"

To this Peter, one of the disciples answered, "Thou art the Christ, the Son of the living God" Matthew 16:16. Peter realized that Jesus is the Lord, the Christ, the Son of the living God, and he confessed his faith. So Jesus said that He would establish His Church on the Son, the everlasting Rock, the only begotten God that Peter had confessed as "the Christ, the Son of the living God."

> "And Jesus answered and said unto him, Blessed art thou, Simon Barjona: for flesh and blood hath not revealed it unto thee, but my Father which is in heaven ... upon this rock I will build my church; and the gates of hell shall not prevail against it." Matthew 16:17-18

> In the rifted Rock I'm resting,
> Safely sheltered, I abide;
> There no foes nor storms molest me,
> While within the cleft I hide.
> Now I'm resting, sweetly resting,
> In the cleft once made for me:

> Jesus, blessed Rock of Ages,
> I will hide myself in Thee.[11]

Upon this rock stands the Church of the Lord.

> "The stone which the builders rejected, the same is become the head of the corner."
>
> Matthew 21:42

Jesus Christ is this head of the corner, the Holy Rock, upon which the Church of God stands. Each of the believers becomes a member of His body and thus we are being built up, one stone upon another to form the holy temple of which the foundation stone is Jesus.

> "John bare witness of him, and cried out, saying, this was he of whom I spake, He that cometh after me is preferred before me: for he was before me."
>
> John 1:15

John the Baptist was born before Jesus, but he said that Jesus was before him. He meant that Jesus had existed even before time.

> "And of his fulness have all we received, and grace for grace. For the law was given by Moses, but grace and truth came by Jesus Christ."
>
> John 1:16-17

"[T]he law was given by Moses." When we consider the Old Testament as a whole, we can see that the law and commandments given to the Jews were all part of the preparations leading up to the birth of Christ. The five books of Moses bore witness to the Christ, and so did the prophets. Thus John chapter 1 verse 14 is very precise when it says, "the Word was made flesh."

"[T]he law was given by Moses."

These are words that every Jew will be able to understand. We, too, as Gentiles can well understand what this is saying, if we read the Old Testament carefully.

"[G]race and truth came by Jesus Christ."

Through Jesus Christ, we are able to praise God's grace, and come to see that Jesus Christ is the truth, the true light, and the true way.

> "No one hath seen God at any time; the only begotten Son, which is in the bosom of the Father, he hath declared him." John 1:18

The only begotten Son. This is Jesus Christ, the one in whom we believe. Step by step we gradually grope our way closer to Jesus. Man-made statues with eyes of gemstones and bodies covered with gold may dazzle our eyes, but no matter how magnificent these man-made idols may be, they cannot give us life.

"[T]he only begotten Son, which is in the bosom of the Father," is Jesus Christ. He is the Son of God, God's Word of life, who was brought into this world in accordance with the prophecies of the Old Testament. If we believe in Him as our Savior and live through faith in Him, we can come ever closer to Him. Also, if we draw nearer to the Bible in our daily lives, the faith will arise in us that will enable us to rely on Him all the more.

4

The Lamb of God, Who Taketh Away the Sin of the World

John 1:19-42

"I am the voice of one crying in the wilderness, Make straight the way of the Lord, as said the prophet Esaias."
John the Baptist was the man who came to break down and plough the hardened hearts of men, in order to prepare them so that the seed of God's word might be properly sown there. John the Baptist saw Jesus as the Lamb of God who takes away the sin of the world.

John 1:19-42

[19] And this is the record of John, when the Jews sent priests and Levites from Jerusalem to ask him, Who art thou?

[20] And he confessed, and denied not; but confessed, I am not the Christ.

[21] And they asked him, What then? Art thou Elias? And he saith, I am not. Art thou that prophet? And he answered, No.

[22] Then said they unto him, Who art thou? that we may give an answer to them that sent us. What sayest thou of thyself?

[23] He said, I am the voice of one crying in the wilderness, Make straight the way of the Lord, as said the prophet Esaias.

[24] And they which were sent were of the Pharisees. [25] And they asked him, and said unto him, Why baptizest thou then, if thou be not that Christ, nor Elias, neither that prophet?

[26] John answered them, saying, I baptize with water: but there standeth one among you, whom ye know not; [27] He it is, who coming after me is preferred before me, whose shoe's latchet I am not worthy to unloose. [28] These things were done in Bethabara beyond Jordan, where John was baptizing.

[29] The next day John seeth Jesus coming unto him, and saith, Behold the Lamb of God, which taketh away the sin of the world. [30] This is he of whom I said, After me cometh a man which is preferred before me: for he was before me. [31] And I knew him not: but that he should be made manifest to Israel, therefore am I come baptizing with water.

[32] And John bare record, saying, I saw the Spirit descending from heaven like a dove, and it abode upon him. [33] And I knew him not: but he that sent me to baptize with water, the same said unto me, Upon whom thou shalt see the Spirit descending, and remaining on him, the same is he which baptizeth with the Holy Ghost. [34] And I saw, and bare record that this is the Son of God.

[35] Again the next day after John stood, and two of his disciples; [36] and looking upon Jesus as he walked, he saith, Behold the Lamb of God!

[37] And the two disciples heard him speak, and they followed Jesus. [38] Then Jesus turned, and saw them following, saith unto them, What

seek ye? They said unto him, Rabbi, (which is to say, being interpreted, Master,) where dwellest thou?

⁳⁹He saith unto them, Come and see. They came and saw where he dwelt, and abode with him that day: for it was about the tenth hour.

⁴⁰One of the two which heard John speak, and followed him, was Andrew, Simon Peter's brother. ⁴¹He first findeth his own brother Simon, and saith unto him, We have found the Messias, which is, being interpreted, the Christ. ⁴²And he brought him to Jesus. And when Jesus beheld him, he said, Thou art Simon the son of Jona: thou shalt be called Cephas, which is by interpretation, A stone.

Who Art Thou?

John chapter 1 from verse 19 begins with the scene in which the priests and Levites came to ask John the Baptist to identify himself. These days, we can satisfy our curiosity and broaden our knowledge through such sources as libraries, bookstores, or the Internet. These were not to be found in biblical times, however, so if anyone had a question, he had to find someone who might be considered a teacher and ask him in person.

The priests and Levites wanted to know once and for all who John the Baptist really was, so they sent men to him to find out. These men listened to John's words and then they asked him, "Who on earth are you?"

"Who art thou?"

Have you ever stood in front of a mirror and asked yourself, "Who are you?"

"Who are you?" This is the question.

When they asked John the Baptist, "Who art thou?" his answer was simple. He said several times, "I am not." When other people flatter us, we like to hear what they say, even if we know it is not true. When these people came to John the Baptist and asked him who he was, he could have said, "Who do you think I am?" and pretended to be the Christ. This, however, was not John's attitude at all.

"And this is the record of John, when the Jews sent priests and Levites from Jerusalem to ask him, Who art thou? And he confessed, and denied not; but confessed, I am not the Christ."   John 1:19-20

John did not pretend to be the Christ, did he? On the contrary, he flatly denied it, making his point plain with a few simple words: "I am not the Christ."

> "And they asked him, What then? Art thou Elias? And he saith, I am not. Art thou that prophet? And he answered, No. Then said they unto him, Who art thou? that we may give an answer to them that sent us. What sayest thou of thyself?" John 1:21-22

This Elias was the prophet Elijah who lived in Old Testament times. When they asked John if he was Elijah, he said that he was not. Throughout history, many people have claimed to be the Christ, but none of them has ever risen from the dead; they have all died and returned to the dust of the ground.

Let's consider here what was in the heart of John the Baptist. He was born six months before Jesus, but he was very well aware of his position. He made it clear that he was not the Christ. The men who had been sent from Jerusalem became very frustrated as they questioned John, so they asked him to give them a clear answer that they could give to the elders who had sent them.

> "He said, I am the voice of one crying in the wilderness, Make straight the way of the Lord, as said the prophet Esaias." John 1:23

Once again, John's answer was simple. He quoted from the Old Testament prophet, Isaiah, as he said, "I am the voice of one crying in the wilderness, Make straight the way of the Lord." He had come to make straight the way of the Lord. You might say that he came to carry out the work of a bulldozer. He came to break down and plough over the hardened hearts of men, in order to prepare them so that the seed of God's word might be properly sown there. He preached repentance and his powerful sermon pierced the hearts of his listeners.

There Standeth One Among You

When certain tax-gatherers came to John and asked him:

"Master, what shall we do?"

He answered:

"Exact no more than that which is appointed you."

Then some soldiers asked him what they should do, and he said:

"Do violence to no man, neither accuse any falsely; and be content with your wages."

In a very simple and precise way, John the Baptist addressed, one by one, the matters that troubled the consciences of these individuals.[1]

At the back of the crowd, however, there were faultfinding teachers of the law. This was true of those who came and said, "Who art thou? That we may give an answer to them that sent us" John 1:22, and also of those who resisted John's words, proudly pointing out that they were descendants of Abraham and that they had adhered strictly to the law. So John expressed his point more precisely, saying:

> "Bring forth therefore fruits worthy of repentance, and begin not to say within yourselves, We have Abraham to our father: for I say unto you, that God is able of these stones to raise up children unto Abraham."
>
> Luke 3:8

John the Baptist preached repentance, urging them to change their way of thinking. He told them that not all the descendants of Abraham would enter the kingdom of heaven.

> "And they which were sent were of the Pharisees. And they asked him, and said unto him, Why baptizest thou then, if thou be not that Christ, nor Elias, neither that prophet?"
>
> John 1:25

Now they asked him another question. "By what authority are you baptizing?" Instead of answering this question, however, John said something quite unexpected.

> "John answered them, saying, I baptize with water: but there standeth one among you, whom ye know not; He it is, who coming after me is preferred before me, whose shoe's latchet I am not worthy to unloose. These things were done in Bethabara beyond Jordan, where John was baptizing." John 1:26-28

John said that he baptized only with water. He then indicated that there was a particular Person standing amongst them, whom they did not know. He drew their attention to the fact that there was someone of note amongst the crowd. John the Baptist had come to bear witness of the Christ and he sensed that the Christ had now appeared.

> "He it is, who coming after me is preferred before me, whose shoe's latchet I am not worthy to unloose." John 1:27

> "[W]hose shoe's latchet I am not worthy to unloose."

How good it would be to be able to live every day with such an attitude.

In biblical times, the Jews wore sandals with the soles made of leather or wood. Straps came up from each side of the soles and wrapped around the heels. They would walk the parched desert roads in this kind of sandal. The intense sunlight beat down, completely drying up the soil so that the dust would fly up with every step. If just one horse were to gallop by, an entire village would be covered by a cloud of dust.

When a visitor came from far away, the first thing a host would do was bring out a bowl of water and wash his guest's feet. Untying the straps of the guest's sandals and washing his feet was considered the height of courtesy and the greatest welcoming gesture. This was the custom at that time. It must have been really good to receive such a welcome. The Jews at that time treated their guests with such great courtesy that a visitor did not even have to wash his own feet. Also, when the master of a house had been out and returned home, his servant would hurry to untie his sandals for him.

John the Baptist, however, said he was not worthy even to stand in the position of a servant to this Man who had now come. How great and overwhelming could this Man have been to have made John feel unworthy to stand before Him even in the lowliest of positions? John said that he was not worthy even to untie the straps of His sandals. He told the crowd that this great Man was coming and was indeed already standing amongst them.

The Lamb of God

The true Light had come and He was there among them.[2] Even though the people at that time saw Jesus, they did not recognize who He was. An electric light or the light from the sun can shine on several people at one time, but the true Light in the Bible is different. Knowing this Light is a personal matter for the individual. We need to come to know this Light individually; we need to realize the truth individually; and we need to believe individually. As individuals we need to receive this Light as our Savior, and as individuals we need to make Him our Lord.

There is a hymn that says:

> Christ, thy Lord is waiting now,
> Let Him in, let Him in.[3]

The true Light is waiting to be received, the light that enlightens every man.

Jesus was there amongst all these individuals and yet they did not know it. Why didn't they know it? They were unable to recognize the Son of God. John the Baptist did not know Him personally either, but John knew who He was and recognized Him when He came forward to be baptized.

> "The next day John seeth Jesus coming unto him, and saith, Behold the Lamb of God, which taketh away the sin of the world. This is he of whom I said, After me cometh a man which is preferred before me: for he was before me. And I knew him not: but that he should be made manifest to Israel, therefore am I come baptizing with water. And John bare record, saying, I saw the Spirit descending from heaven like a dove, and it abode upon him. And I knew him not: but he that sent me to baptize with water, the same said unto me, Upon whom thou shalt see the Spirit descending, and remaining on him, the same is he which baptizeth with the Holy Ghost. And I saw, and bare record that this is the Son of God." John 1:29-34

As John was baptizing with water, he saw the Holy Spirit descending upon Jesus, so he knew that this Man was the Son of God. When John said, "After me cometh a man which is preferred before me: for he was before me," it meant that this Man existed from the beginning. Verse 29 of this chapter is extremely important.

> "The next day John seeth Jesus coming unto him, and saith, Behold the Lamb of God, which taketh away the sin of the world." John 1:29

The expression, "the Lamb of God," appears twice in the first chapter of John's Gospel. The first time John identified Jesus in this way was when he saw Jesus coming out of the wilderness and said, "Behold the Lamb of God, which taketh away the sin of the world" John 1:29. The other time was when John saw Jesus walking along and said, "Behold the Lamb of God!" John 1:36. There is something for us to think about here.

Many people had gathered in the wilderness to listen to John the Baptist's sermon, but then the Lamb of God appeared. These were people who had spent a lot of time studying and listening to the Old Testament scriptures. As a result, they were waiting for the coming of the Messiah, in other words, the Christ, and they believed that He would come. Even so, when John saw Jesus coming to him and cried out, saying, "Behold the Lamb of God, which taketh away the sin of the world," those who were standing by did not know what John meant.

When the Israelites came out of Egypt, long before this, they slaughtered a lamb and daubed its blood on the doorposts and lintels of their houses. Thus they avoided God's judgment at that time and none of them died, even though all the first-born sons of Egypt were killed. Let's take a look at Exodus chapter 12 and see what kind of animal the Israelites slaughtered when they came out of Egypt.

> "Your lamb shall be without blemish, a male of the first year: ye shall take it from the sheep, or from the goats." Exodus 12:5

What does it say the Israelites were to offer as a sacrifice for their sins? They were told to offer a lamb or a goat. It says that the lamb was to be without blemish and a year old. This lamb is a shadow of Christ who went silently to the slaughter. There is a hymn that says:

> I'm redeemed by the blood of the Lamb.[4]

The goat here presents an image of Jesus Christ as He took upon Himself all our sins; the sins of all mankind. He was completely covered in our sins.

As we read through the Old Testament, we come across an animal that was sent out into the wilderness. In their sacrifices, the Jews would offer before God, the blood of a lamb, but they would also bring a goat. The priest would lay his hands on the head of the goat and thus the sins of the sinner were transferred to the animal. A man was then appointed to take the goat out into the wilderness and release it there. The wilderness was inhabited by all kinds of wild beasts who would soon devour the goat and that would be the end of both the animal and the sins it bore. Let's turn now to Leviticus chapter 16.

> "And Aaron shall cast lots upon the two goats; one lot for the Lord, and the other lot for the scapegoat. And Aaron shall bring the goat upon which the Lord's lot fell, and offer him for a sin offering. But the goat, on which the lot fell to be the scapegoat, shall be presented alive before the Lord, to make an atonement with him, and to let him go for a scapegoat into the wilderness." Leviticus 16:8-10

> "And Aaron shall lay both his hands upon the head of the live goat, and confess over him all the iniquities of the children of Israel, and all their transgressions in all their sins, putting them upon the head of the goat, and shall send him away by the hand of a fit man into the wilderness: and the goat shall bear upon him all their iniquities unto a land not inhabited: and he shall let go the goat in the wilderness." Leviticus 16:21-22

Whom does this goat resemble? It is just like Jesus, isn't it? It is a literary portrait of Jesus, recorded before He was even born. Why is that? The goat resembles Jesus in that all the sins of all the people were transferred to the goat and it was sent out into the wilderness. Who, then, was the "fit man" Leviticus 16:21 who released the goat into the wilderness? John the Baptist was the man who had been standing waiting, and when Jesus appeared in the wilderness, John pointed Him out to the people saying, "Behold the Lamb of God, which taketh away the sin of the world." Jesus appeared in the wilderness as the Lamb of God who took upon Himself the sin of the whole world. When John the Baptist saw Him, Jesus appeared to him as the goat that was to be the scapegoat, because Jesus would take upon Himself all the sins of the world.

He who is Greater than John the Baptist

John the Baptist was the last of the prophets of Old Testament times. He did not come in order to receive the Christ, but purely to bear witness of Him. When John the Baptist, as a prophet, saw the Christ, he saw all the sacrificial lambs, all the sacrifices that had been offered in Old Testament times.

Let's take a look now at John's Gospel chapter 1 verses 35 and 36.

"Again the next day after John stood, and two of his disciples; and looking upon Jesus as he walked, he saith, Behold the Lamb of God!"

John the Baptist says, "Behold," twice in this chapter (verses 29 and 36). Why would he have done this? The first time he was referring to the Christ who is revealed in the Old Testament, the Christ who was prophesied in the Old Testament, the Christ who was to take upon Himself the sins of mankind and go to His death. This is what John the Baptist saw and was indicating when he said, "Behold."

Today, the Bible is complete and everything is recorded there for us. In those days, however, individuals did not have their own personal copies of the scriptures so they needed to hear about the Christ from someone who had actually seen Him. In verse 36, John the Baptist said, "Behold" once more. Here he was no longer indicating the Christ of the Old Testament who had come as a sacrificial offering; he was pointing out the Christ who was physically present and active.

"And looking upon Jesus as he walked, he saith, Behold the Lamb of God!"
John 1:36

This Lamb is the Lord who was to suffer in this world. He appeared here as the One who would be treated with nothing but scorn as He carried out His work in this world only to be put to death at the end. Like a lamb being led to the slaughter, He would walk through the three years of His ministry that would culminate in His death.

Jesus often said, "My hour has not yet come." He said that His hour had not come, and He also spoke of the path He had to take. On one occasion, someone came to Him and said:

"Lord, I will follow thee whithersoever thou goest."　　　Luke 9:57

Jesus replied:

"Foxes have holes, and birds of the air have nests; but the Son of man hath not where to lay his head."　　　Luke 9:58

Jesus had to continue on His path. Where was this path taking Him? There are several instances where the Bible says that Jesus went up to Jerusalem. We can see how He was gradually approaching the city, and His last steps to Jerusalem took Him to His death, the death of the true sacrificial Lamb.

> Every step He took on His path
> Is filled with His tears and His blood.[5]

In Jesus' every move, He was walking towards His death. Behind every word He said, He was indicating that He was going to His death. Only then could He say at the end, "It is finished."

The light is there so that we might see. In order that His light might shine, Jesus not only existed as the word but He also fulfilled the word to the letter.

"But these are written that ye might believe that Jesus is the Christ, the Son of God; and that believing ye might have life through his name."　　　John 20:31

Here we have the purpose for which the Bible was written. It was written in order that we might believe that Jesus is the Christ, the Son of God, and thus receive eternal life. So when John the Baptist first saw Jesus John 1:29, he saw Him as the Christ who appeared in the wilderness to bear the sins of the world in accordance with the Old Testament prophesies. When John saw Him again, however, and said, "Behold the Lamb of God" John 1:36, he saw Jesus as the Lamb walking the rugged path to His wretched death on the cross.

As we read the Bible, we may sympathize deeply with Jesus, as He carried the cross on His back, step by step, whipped by the Roman soldiers along the way. When we see this kind of scene in a movie, we may even be moved to tears. When John the Baptist saw Jesus, he saw a Man who was soon to die. This was the Jesus that John indicated as being the Christ. So John led the disciples whom he had taught and trained to Jesus and told them that Jesus was the Son of God.

Come and See

> "And the two disciples heard him speak, and they followed Jesus. Then Jesus turned, and saw them following, and saith unto them, What seek ye? They said unto him, Rabbi, (which is to say, being interpreted, Master,) where dwellest thou? He saith unto them, Come and see. They came and saw where he dwelt, and abode with him that day: for it was about the tenth hour." John 1:37-39

When John's disciples heard their teacher testify, "Behold the Lamb of God," they followed Jesus. Jesus saw the two people following Him, so He asked them, "What seek ye?" He was asking them what they wanted, so they said to Him, "Rabbi, ... where dwellest thou?"

The Lamb of God, Who Taketh Away the Sin of the World

Jesus' answer was simple: "Come and see."

Let's think about this. There are many places in this world for us to go and see, aren't there? Perhaps you know this song:

> Mid pleasures and palaces though we may roam,
> Be it ever so humble, there's no place like home.[6]

There is no place like home, but many people do not see how good it is to be at home. When we think about it, it would seem that we have been born into this world in order to see something.

We also use this word "see" in the sense of trying or finding something out. We see what something looks like. We see what it is like to sit down, stand up, or lie down. We see what it is like to get married. There are so many things for us to see. Our spirits have come into the world, clothed in the flesh, to experience something here. We came to feel something and to know something. We were born to learn and grasp something. Yet, man is the most pitiful being there is.

> "All things are full of labor; man cannot utter it: the eye is not satisfied with seeing, nor the ear filled with hearing."   Ecclesiastes 1:8

We may look and look, and we may see everything under the sun, yet we will still not be satisfied. What Zacchaeus saw from the top of the tree was different. Nothing can compare with Jesus, as Zacchaeus saw Him on that day. Zacchaeus was short so he climbed up a sycamore tree in order to be able to see Jesus. As he looked down from the top of the tree, He found Jesus looking up at him. Then, to his great surprise, Jesus called out to him and said:

> "Zacchaeus, make haste, and come down."   Luke 19:5

Madness Is in Their Heart While They Live

No matter where we may go looking in this world, we will not find true happiness anywhere. When I was about five or six years old, if I saw a rainbow in the sky, I thought that the end of it must be in a stream somewhere. So I would run with the neighborhood children until the sun went down, stubbornly trying to find the end of the rainbow, but we never found it. Later I read an essay entitled, "The End of the Rainbow," and there I found that we were not the only ones who had run off in search of the rainbow's end. Where can we find the happiness that people seek as we sought the end of the rainbow as children?

"Come and see."

The lives of the people who heard these words recorded here in John chapter 1 were completely changed. Through the Bible, we can follow their tracks as they walked into a new future as a result of listening to these words. If we do not follow their example, even though we may see all there is to see in this world, and hear all there is to hear, we will remain among the pathetic ranks of those who have not been able to find the foundation of true happiness.

God's word, however, has come to us as the light, and we have been given life. This life has become ours, and through this life, we have come to breathe the breath of eternity, so that when we come to the end of our lives on this earth, we may go to a holy death.

Have you ever thought about your own death? I sometimes wonder what my reaction would be if some day I was suddenly told that I had cancer and only had a short time to live. Would I spend each day in tears, or would I put up a fight, determined not to die? Or perhaps I would just give up in despair. Then again, if I were to spend that same period of time in good health and then suddenly die in a traffic

The Lamb of God, Who Taketh Away the Sin of the World

accident, what would be the attitude in my heart as I lived out those days? Would I just live my life without thinking about it? My greatest fear is expressed in the verse that says:

> "[M]adness is in their heart while they live, and after that they go to the dead."
> Ecclesiastes 9:3

Let me tell you about a scene I witnessed a long time ago that still remains vivid in my mind.

A young man was running hard to catch his bus, but just as he got to the bus stop, the doors of the bus closed and the bus drew away. I then watched as the young man stamped his feet impatiently, looking at his watch every few moments, urgency written all over his face. It occurred to me that there was not much difference between the image of that man and my life in general.

It is the same for all of us. We may enjoy ourselves when we go to a movie or some other place of entertainment, but when it is over we soon forget all about it.

What do we have in our lives in this world?

Suppose there are just two roles in a play: that of a king and that of a doorkeeper. If the doorkeeper were the main character, which role would you prefer? Let's say there are two roles in another play: that of a handsome well-dressed person, and that of a poor leper. If the leper were the hero of the play, which role would be the better of the two?

Where do we find the greatest happiness? Happiness definitely does not come from outside of us, does it? The Bible talks about historical events, incidents that actually occurred in the past, but it contains more than that; there are also verses that emit the light of life.

"In the beginning was the Word, and the Word was with God, and the Word was God. The same was in the beginning with God. All things were made by him; and without him was not any thing made that was made. In him was life; and the life was the light of men."

John 1:1-4

When the light of God's word shines on us, we forget all our worries and cares and we begin to sing hymns.

> Jesus comes with pow'r to gladden,
> When love shines in,
> Ev'ry life that woe can sadden,
> When love shines in.[7]

We should always hope for our lives to be like this. We should have this kind of confidence. Happiness is not to be found anywhere else. No matter what our circumstances may be, whether we are distressed, sad, or lonely, and no matter where we are, when we stay close to the words of the Bible, our troubles disappear. This is because God's light then shines into our hearts, just as light shines into darkness.

They Came and Saw Where He Dwelt and Abode with Him That Day

Jesus said, "Come and see." Each one of us needs to give this commandment deep consideration, "Come and see."

"They came and saw where he dwelt, and abode with him that day: for it was about the tenth hour."

John 1:39

By our modern calculations, this would have been about four o'clock in the afternoon.[8]

Who responded to Jesus' words, when He said, "Come and see"? We have accepted Jesus. We have believed in Jesus. The true Light came into the world and shone on every man that comes into the world. He came to each individual and became the Christ to each individual. The place that Jesus told them to come and see is the place where man can meet Christ. It is not only these disciples who saw Jesus; we, too, can come and see Him. We, too, can meet Him.

"They came and saw where he dwelt, and abode with him that day."

There are some people who have read verses like this in the Bible and yet they think that since Jesus has now ascended into heaven, they must wait to meet Him at His Second Coming.

When they sing the hymn that says, "'Tis so sweet to walk with Jesus, step by step and day by day,"[9] it seems as though Jesus is right beside them. Then they sing another hymn about waiting for the Lord's return, and He suddenly seems to be a long way away. This is strange, isn't it?

There is a hymn that includes the words:

> I'm rejoicing night and day,
> As I walk the pilgrim way,
> For the hand of God in all my life I see.[10]

How does it feel to know that the Lord is always with us? The disciples were the first people to meet Jesus, follow Him around and spend time with Him. Therefore they wrote about, "that . . . which we have heard, which we have seen with our eyes, which we have looked upon, and our hands have handled" 1 John 1:1. The disciples touched Him, they leaned on Him, and they talked with Him. It is true that our position is different from that of the disciples, but when Jesus says, "Come and see," and we follow Him, we come to see the world in a different light as we look at things through His eyes.

> "One of the two who heard John speak, and followed him, was Andrew, Simon Peter's brother. He first findeth his own brother Simon, and saith unto him, We have found the Messias, which is, being interpreted, the Christ. And he brought him to Jesus. And when Jesus beheld him, he said, Thou art Simon the son of Jona: thou shall be called Cephas, which is by interpretation, a Stone."
>
> John 1:40-42

Andrew was Peter's younger brother, and he told Peter about Jesus. So Peter came to see Jesus. Jesus looked at Peter and said, "Thou art Simon the son of Jona: thou shall be called Cephas." He gave Peter this name that means "rock." Even though Andrew was the one who evangelized to Peter, he himself was not given a special name, whereas Peter was given the name of Cephas. Even so, Andrew was not in the least concerned about being usurped in this way by his brother. He was not a person to be jealous about such matters.

Let's take a look at Andrew's position here. If we name Jesus' disciples one by one in a list, we might say, "Peter, Andrew, James, John, Philip and Bartholomew, Thomas and Matthew the publican." The names both of Peter and Andrew appear in the list, but it always seems to be Peter to who comes to the fore. Nevertheless, it seems that Andrew was not the type of person who minded being put in the second place.

No matter where we may be or what we may do, we should always bear in mind that we are living with God, and that He is with us. When Jesus said , "Come and see," where did they go? We must go to the Bible and see; we must stay close to the Bible and be with Christ. Aren't these the matters that should take priority in our hearts?

5

Those Who Followed Jesus

John 1:43-51

Wherever the gospel has been preached over the past two
thousand years, everyone, from peasant to king, who has ever
heeded Jesus' call to "Follow Me," has taken the right path.
This is an enormous step to take.
It is through this calling, "Follow Me," that Christianity has arisen
throughout the world.
Jesus' words, "Follow Me," continue to flow
even through our lives today.

John 1:43-51

⁴³The day following Jesus would go forth into Galilee, and findeth Philip, and saith unto him, Follow me.

⁴⁴Now Philip was of Bethsaida, the city of Andrew and Peter. ⁴⁵Philip findeth Nathanael, and saith unto him, We have found him, of whom Moses in the law, and the prophets, did write, Jesus of Nazareth, the son of Joseph.

⁴⁶And Nathanael said unto him, Can there any good thing come out of Nazareth? Philip saith unto him, Come and see.

⁴⁷Jesus saw Nathanael coming to him, and saith of him, Behold an Israelite indeed, in whom is no guile!

⁴⁸Nathanael saith unto him, Whence knowest thou me? Jesus answered and said unto him, Before that Philip called thee, when thou wast under the fig tree, I saw thee.

⁴⁹Nathanael answered and saith unto him, Rabbi, thou art the Son of God; thou art the King of Israel.

⁵⁰Jesus answered and said unto him, Because I said unto thee, I saw thee under the fig tree, believest thou? thou shalt see greater things than these.

⁵¹And he saith unto him, Verily, verily, I say unto you, Hereafter ye shall see heaven open, and the angels of God ascending and descending upon the Son of man.

Where He Leads Me I Will Follow

In this passage, there are two points in particular that we need keep in mind: what Jesus said to the disciples when He first met them, and how we felt in our hearts when we ourselves were first touched by the gospel.

> "The day following Jesus would go forth into Galilee, and findeth Philip, and saith unto him, Follow me." John 1:43

We often sing the hymn that includes the line, "Where He leads me I will follow," but do we sing these words without thinking about them? Or do we really feel in our hearts that we have been called to follow the Lord? In other words, do we just sing that we will follow Jesus when in fact He has never told us to? Or when you came to know God's love, did you feel compelled to spread the gospel to others even though no one told you to do this? Did you feel this desire? Did your conscience tell you this is what you should do, even though you did not know how to do it?

> I can hear my Savior calling,
> "Take thy cross and follow, follow Me."
> Where He leads me I will follow.[1]

The day comes when this attitude arises in our hearts. Many people have set out to spread the gospel on the basis of this experience, only to encounter insults and accusations of insanity and heresy. At times, people have brought this upon themselves because they go about things in the wrong way or they are misunderstood by those to whom they try to speak. Whatever the case, from the day we come to believe in Jesus, new thoughts definitely arise in our hearts, thoughts that are not our own. This was not just the case for Philip; it happens to every one of us when we come to realize the love of God.

> O happy day, that fixed my choice,
> On Thee my Savior and my God,
> He drew me and I followed on,
> Charmed to confess the voice divine.
> Happy day, happy day,
> When Jesus washed my sins away.[2]

Without a doubt, there is a day that marks a new beginning for us. Just as on that day we hear a certain calling in our hearts, when Philip first met Jesus, the Lord spoke to him directly, saying, "Follow Me." Philip heard these words and followed Jesus, but his situation was different from ours.

Jesus' ministry lasted for the three years leading up to His crucifixion. He began to preach at the age of about thirty and was crucified at the age of about 33.

It was at the beginning of His ministry that Jesus told Philip to follow Him. So Philip heard these words three years before the crucifixion. He looked to the future and believed. We, on the other hand, are able to look back to the crucifixion that has already happened in the past and believe.

In more than one passage in John's Gospel, we find Jesus telling His disciples that when the Holy Spirit of truth came, He would bring to their remembrance all that He had said to them.[3] It was before the Holy Spirit had come that Philip came to know Jesus. He knew Jesus according to the flesh; he heard His words, and traveled around with Him. Nevertheless, he did not yet know the significance of the crucifixion, or that Jesus was to die and rise again from the dead. He was unclear on all of these points and yet he believed in Jesus, followed Him, and entrusted himself to Him.

In the Gospels of Matthew, Mark, Luke, and John, we are able to read all about what happened in the course of the three years of

Jesus' ministry. We can see what the disciples did and how they lived. So our situation is quite the opposite of that of Philip. As we follow Jesus, we believe the facts that have already been accomplished.

Follow Me

I often think about why it was that Peter began to sink when he walked on the water. He was walking on the water toward Jesus. He did actually walk on the water, didn't he? But as soon as he began to think about himself, he also began to sink.[4] As long as we are in the flesh, we are weak and so we make mistakes as did Peter and Thomas. As human beings, we are clearly very weak. When we come to believe the events that occurred two thousand years ago, this comes about by the power of the Holy Spirit that we receive at that time.

> I know not how the Spirit moves,
> Convincing men of sin,
> Revealing Jesus through the Word,
> Creating faith in Him.
> But "I know whom I have believed,
> And am persuaded that He is able
> To keep that which I've committed
> Unto Him against that day."[5]

"I know not how the Spirit moves, convincing men of sin, revealing Jesus through the Word, creating faith in Him." The writer of this hymn was not saying that she really did not know; she was trying to write of her inexpressible gratitude and asking why Jesus should go so far as to die for a lowly person such as herself.

We have come to know and believe the great work that Jesus accomplished, but it is not for us to follow Jesus around in the flesh as the disciples did. Just as Philip followed Jesus around for three years from the time he first met Him, after we come to realize the truth of the gospel, all that is left for us is to do is follow Jesus by reading the New Testament and living our lives accordingly.

Imagine what emotions must have surged through Philip when he heard Jesus saying to him, "Follow me." As soon as Philip heard these words, he dropped everything and followed Jesus. We can see this as an indication of his pure and uncomplicated heart.

If this had happened today, it probably would have caused an outrage. The members of his family would have come to him and got right down to the point, yelling at him and saying, "What do you think you are doing? Who is going to support your family? Are you going to follow that Man? He doesn't even have a job!" They would have started fighting with one another over this matter. When this Man suddenly appeared out of the blue, however, and said, "Follow Me," Philip did not ask him how much his salary would be, how he would be able to support himself, or what he was going to eat. He asked no such questions; he simply followed Jesus.

Before we go on, let's take a moment to consider this simple faith that Philip had. In a way, you might say that Jesus was rather harsh when He said to this disciple, "Follow Me." How could He take responsibility for these young men as He told them to leave their homes and go with Him? Nonetheless, wherever the gospel has been preached over the past two thousand years, everyone, from peasant to king, who has ever heeded Jesus' call to "Follow Me," has taken the right path. We know that this is an enormous step to take.

A tremendous responsibility lay behind these words, "Follow Me." It was not just out of a passing whim that Jesus told Philip to follow Him; this command was far from ordinary. As we continue our study, we will be taking a closer look at how Philip went about following Jesus. The problem is that many people in the world do not have anyone or anything in the world to follow. When I was younger, there were times when I, too, wished there had been someone to tell me to follow them. The more I entertained such thoughts, the more I found my heart being led along by the fascinating Personage who appears in the Bible.

Man's basic way of thinking is the same in no matter which age he may live. The only differences lie in the degree of development of civilization and cultural levels. All people have the same selfish desires, thoughts, and ambitions. Yet it is the life of one particular Man that seems to draw us along, a Man who appeared quite suddenly, out of the blue.

"Follow Me."

Was this an ordinary thing to say? When Philip heard these words, what would it have been that motivated him to obey? Was he seeking money or fame? What would have been his reason? Jesus probably did not appear to have much to offer in human terms. The Bible says that Jesus had "no form nor comeliness; and when we shall see him, there is no beauty that we should desire him" Isaiah 53:2.

Nevertheless, Philip devoted his whole life to following Jesus. He had a complete change of occupation, giving up the work he had always done and becoming an evangelist. There were no theological schools in those days; Philip simply came to Jesus and learned by listening to Him. There was one thing, however, of which Philip was absolutely certain; he knew that Jesus was the Son of God, the One of whom the prophets had spoken. So it was not that Philip had familiarized himself with some learned theory; he simply told others who Jesus was.

This is something that everyone needs to know: who Jesus was. His name is widely known, but if we are not careful we may secularize it, just listing it along with all the other names to be found in this world.

Jesus' call to follow Him is extremely meaningful. It is through this calling, "Follow Me," that Christianity has arisen throughout the world. Jesus' words, "Follow Me," were heard at the beginning of the history of Christianity but they did not stop there; they continue to flow even through our lives today. Jesus did not say, "Follow Me if you feel like it. It's up to you." He said very precisely, "Follow Me."

We Have Found Him

Jesus has brought us to believe in Him and He has sown within us a sense of responsibility towards others so that we feel that we, too, must bring them to believe. Here, Philip also experienced this within his spirit.

> "The day following Jesus would go forth into Galilee, and findeth Philip, and saith unto him, Follow me. Now Philip was of Bethsaida, the city of Andrew and Peter. Philip findeth Nathanael, and saith unto him, We have found him, of whom Moses in the law, and the prophets, did write, Jesus of Nazareth, the son of Joseph."
>
> John 1:43-45

This is often the way that we react as well. We usually begin by trying to spread the gospel to those who are closest to us—immediate family and friends.

Philip went to find Nathanael[6] and said, "We have found him, of whom Moses in the law, and the prophets, did write, Jesus of Nazareth, the son of Joseph." This is very interesting. Philip's method of spreading the gospel to Nathanael was very simple.

You have probably seen people standing in the streets handing out pamphlets, telling people to believe in Jesus if they do not want to go to hell. Philip's method of spreading the gospel, however, was far more sophisticated. His words were concise and accurate: "We have found Him, of whom Moses in the law, and the prophets, did write." In his excitement, he went on to say that the Messiah was the Nazarene, the son of Joseph. In reply, Nathanael said:

"Can there any good thing come out of Nazareth?"

So Philip said to him, "Come and see."[7]

Nathanael's words were also very simple: "Can anything good come out of Nazareth? Are you trying to tell me the great prophet is the son of Joseph from Nazareth?"

Sometimes these days we may find that people from one region of a country do not get on too well with those from another region. The enmity that the Jews felt towards the inhabitants of the region in which Nazareth lay, however, was quite another story. Nazareth was in the land of Israel, but so many Jews in that area had married gentiles and there were so many people of mixed blood that the Jews in other regions considered Nazareth to be virtually a gentile land. The orthodox Jews treated the people from this region with complete disdain. It was quite different from the area around Bethlehem or Jerusalem, the home of the more patriotic and legalistic Jews who adhered strictly to the laws and traditions of their nation. It was for this reason that Nathanael said, "Can there any good thing come out of Nazareth?"[8]

Can there Any Good Thing Come out of Nazareth?

> "And Jesus himself began to be about thirty years of age, being (as was supposed) the son of Joseph." Luke 3:23

People thought that Jesus was the son of Joseph, but whose son did God know Him to be? He was the Son of God.

When it says here it was supposed that He was the son of Joseph, it means that actually He was not. Philip thought that Jesus was the son of Joseph. He also thought that He was the Messiah of whom it was written in the Old Testament scriptures, but at this stage, he would not have dared to suggest that Jesus was the Son of God. He might have had an idea that this was the case, but his mind was full of doubts since this was before Jesus' crucifixion.

Nathanael was a man who adhered strictly to the law and He was well versed in the scriptures and the writings of the prophets. In his eyes, Philip probably appeared to be somewhat naïve and so he said to him, "Can there any good thing come out of Nazareth?" Philip approached Nathanael and tried to persuade him that Jesus was the Christ, but he soon ran out of things to say. So then what did he do? He said, "Come and see." His method was a good one. If he had tried to force Nathanael to believe, he would have failed, but instead he told him to come and see and Nathanael came to Jesus.

> "Jesus saw Nathanael coming to him, and saith of him, Behold an Israelite indeed, in whom is no guile!" John 1:47

Nathanael went to Jesus because Philip had urged him to do so, but he still had doubts in his heart. Perhaps he thought, "I'd better go and see what this is all about. Who is this person called Jesus? Philip has been spending time with these uneducated fishermen like Peter and it looks like they have been leading him astray. But perhaps I'd better go and see for myself." Perhaps he went in order to size Jesus up or to criticize Him. We do not know exactly what he was thinking, but in any case, he did not just ignore what Philip said; he went to see Jesus.

Even as he was on his way, Jesus saw him first and spoke about him. Jesus was not concerned about the doubts and criticisms in Nathanael's heart; He could see that it contained no guile.

Nathanael said that nothing good could come out of Nazareth because, as far as he knew, there were no Old Testament prophecies that said that the Messiah would come from that city.

We should not really be surprised as his misunderstanding. Jesus was conceived in Nazareth, but He was born in Bethlehem. He lived in Egypt for a short time when He was a very young child and then He moved to Nazareth. Nathanael was convinced that no great person could come from Nazareth. He was a person who knew how to question and would not just believe blindly. As he looked further into this matter, he came to believe.

Nathanael had the writings of the Old Testament in mind as he spoke of Jesus, but Jesus just saw Nathanael exactly as he was. He saw that Nathanael was an Israelite with an honest heart and an intelligent mind. When Philip told him about Jesus, he did not just accept every word he heard and agree to go and meet this great man. In his heart he was tempted to reject what he was hearing. Nevertheless, he was ready to take a look and see what this was all about. Jesus knew all of this and said of Nathanael, "Behold, an Israelite indeed, in whom is no guile!"

This must have been quite a shock for Nathanael. How could this Man possibly know him? He had never met Him before, and so he asked Jesus, "Whence knowest thou me?"

> "Nathanael saith unto him, Whence knowest thou me? Jesus answered and said unto him, Before that Philip called thee, when thou wast under the fig tree, I saw thee." John 1:48

Jesus said to him, "Before that Philip called thee, when thou wast under the fig tree, I saw thee." Nathanael must have wondered what fig tree He was talking about and when He had seen him sitting under it. There are many fig trees in Israel. They grow well there since that region enjoys the warm breezes that blow in from the

Mediterranean Sea. Also, not many insects live on fig trees since they dislike the taste of the leaves. In biblical times, the shade of a fig tree provided an ideal place for the godly men of Israel to rest, meditate, or pray. It appears that Nathanael too had been praying under one of the fig trees, and God heard these prayers. So it was that Jesus already knew Nathanael before Nathanael came to Him.

Jesus was God, the One who hears the prayers of men, and He knew every one of Nathanael's movements. This is how He was able to say, "When thou wast under the fig tree, I saw thee."

For Unto Us a Child Is Born

Jesus was particularly interested in the fig tree. On one occasion He said:

> "Now learn a parable of the fig tree; When her branch is yet tender, and putteth forth leaves, ye know that summer is near: So ye in like manner, when ye shall see these things come to pass, know that it is nigh, even at the doors."
>
> Mark 13:28-29

"Learn a parable of the fig tree." Jesus addressed these words to the Jews. The nation of the Israelites has something very much in common with the fig tree. The special characteristic of the fig is that although it bears fruit, it does not bear any blossom. If you cut open an unripe fig, however, you will find the blossom inside it. When this ripens, it becomes a tasty fruit.

So Jesus used the parable of the fig tree when talking about the promise of the redemption of Israel. When the Israelites were in bondage in Egypt too, God raised up Moses secretly like the hidden flower of the fig.

> "Now learn a parable of the fig tree; When his branch is yet tender, and putteth forth leaves, ye know that summer is nigh: So likewise ye,

when ye shall see all these things, know that it is near, even at the doors.".

Matthew 24:32

Long ago there was a time when the Israelites were taken captive to Babylon. From that time on, they were continually under the control of various foreign powers and therefore were unable to restore their nation.

On May 14, 1948, however, Israel was finally declared once more to be an independent nation, and in 1967, they recaptured parts of Jerusalem. It was around 600 BC when the Babylonians took control of Judea, but it was only after a long period of about 2,600 years that the nation of Israel was restored.⁹

This is an extraordinary occurrence. These events give us a clue as to what will happen in the future, just as the Old Testament prophesies told in advance of the birth and coming of the Christ. The Old Testament prophets explained continually about the coming of a King. As an example, let's take a look at what it says in Isaiah chapter 32.

> "Behold, a king shall reign in righteousness, and princes shall rule in judgment. And a man shall be as an hiding place from the wind, and a covert from the tempest; as rivers of water in a dry place, as the shadow of a great rock in a weary land. And the eyes of them that see shall not be dim, and the ears of them that hear shall hearken. The heart also of the rash shall understand knowledge, and the tongue of the stammerers shall be ready to speak plainly."

Isaiah 32:1-4

Who is this talking about? It is Jesus Christ, the Son of God. The Jews, including Nathanael, had been waiting and longing for the Messiah to come and take His throne. In Isaiah chapter 9 verses 6 and 7 it says:

"For unto us a child is born, unto us a son is given: and the government shall be upon his shoulder: and his name shall be called Wonderful, Counsellor, The mighty God, The everlasting Father, The Prince of Peace. Of the increase of his government and peace there shall be no end, upon the throne of David, and upon his kingdom, to order it, and to establish it with judgment and with justice from henceforth even for ever. The zeal of the Lord of hosts will perform this."

Isaiah 9:6-7

Who is this "child" referred to here? He is the King of kings. It was promised in advance that He would come. Now let's take a look at Isaiah chapter 52.

"Behold, my servant shall deal prudently, he shall be exalted and extolled, and be very high. As many were astonied at thee; his visage was so marred more than any man, and his form more than the sons of men: So shall he sprinkle many nations; the kings shall shut their mouths at him: for that which had not been told them shall they see; and that which they had not heard shall they consider." Isaiah 52:13-15

In chapter 9 of Isaiah we read that a Child was to be born, and if we examine His name carefully we find that it says He would be God. Here in chapter 52 it says, "He shall be exalted and extolled, and be very high," and "His visage was so marred more than any man."

In other words, He would be beaten and whipped, and would wear a crown of thorns on His head. His face would be so terribly marred it would be a horror to behold. Such are the prophecies regarding the Christ that were recorded and explained in advance in the Old Testament scriptures just as the letter to the Hebrews tells us: "In the volume of the book it is written of me" Hebrews 10:7.

Thou Art the King of Israel

> "Nathanael answered and saith unto him, Rabbi, thou art the Son of God; thou art the King of Israel."   John 1:49

What was it that Nathanael had now come to realize? He said, "[T]hou art the Son of God; thou art the King of Israel." Is this an ordinary everyday matter? It is difficult enough for us to meet with the president of our own country, let alone the Son of God. You have probably participated in many general elections in your country, but have you ever met the president you have elected? If you were to approach him, you would probably be restrained by guards. Except for a special occasion, it is unlikely that you would be able to meet him.

Nathanael had probably never imagined that he would ever be able to meet the King of Israel, but thanks to Philip's sudden and unexpected evangelizing, he was granted this opportunity.

You are probably familiar with the words of the following hymn:

> Noel, noel, noel, noel,
> Born is the King of Israel.[10]

Who is this King of Israel? He was born in a humble stable, so it was inevitable that He should be treated with contempt. Had Jesus been born in a palace, however, we ordinary people would never be able to be saved. If He had not come in order to die for the sake of ordinary people, how could we have been saved? He humbled Himself, taking the form of a bondservant. He was even treated like an animal, from the day He was born.

It was not by chance that He happened to be born in Bethlehem, just as the prophet Micah had foretold.[11] If you look up the word "Bethlehem" in a dictionary, you will find that it means "house of bread." What is significant about the fact that He was born in a city whose name means "house of bread"? One day, when this Child born in the house of bread had grown to be a Man, He said, "I am the bread of life." This seems to correspond to the basic principle that bread is made in a bread house.

When Nathanael met Jesus, he said, "Rabbi, thou art the Son of God; thou art the King of Israel." He and the other disciples believed that this King would reign on this earth in their time in glorious majesty.

If you read all the way through the four Gospels, you will come across a number of scenes in which the disciples are found recklessly vying with one another to secure the more exalted positions for themselves. On one occasion, the mother of the sons of Zebedee, two of the disciples, asked Jesus to seat her sons one on His left and the other on His right when He came into His kingdom.

> "And he said unto her, What wilt thou? She saith unto him, Grant that these my two sons may sit, the one on thy right hand, and the other on the left, in thy kingdom."　　　　　　　　　　Matthew 20:21

Even when Jesus had been crucified, had risen from the dead and was about to ascend into heaven, the disciples were still thinking the same thing as they asked Him, "Lord, wilt thou at this time restore again the kingdom to Israel?" Not long before this, Jesus had been crucified. Then He had risen from the dead and for the following forty days He had taught and explained everything to them, but still they thought that perhaps now He would reign as King over Israel. In their hearts, this is what they were ready and waiting for. The Jews had crucified Him. They had killed Him, and yet He had risen from the dead. What more was needed to qualify Him as King of Israel?

"Lord, wilt thou at this time restore again the kingdom to Israel?"

Acts 1:6

Do you think this Man who had risen from the dead would allow Himself to be made king of a world of such petty beings who were destined for death and decay? Why should such a worthy Personage spend His time tethered in this way? He had not come to be King over this trivial world. He had to leave this world in order to become the true King.

Since Jesus was now so full of life, having actually risen from the dead, however, the disciples thought they should make Him their King right away and not miss their chance. He had been teaching them thoroughly for forty days, explaining everything to them, and now He was just about to ascend into heaven, ten days before the day of Pentecost. As He spoke to the disciples at this time, they asked Him about the restoration of Israel. They thought that the kingdom of heaven would be revealed right away. So Jesus said to them:

> "And he said unto them, It is not for you to know the times or the seasons, which the Father hath put in his own power. But ye shall receive power, after that the Holy Ghost is come upon you: and ye shall be witnesses unto me both in Jerusalem, and in all Judaea, and in Samaria, and unto the uttermost part of the earth." Acts 1:7-8

These verses are taken from the Acts of the Apostles, a book which, as its name suggests, contains an account of the activities of the apostles. It was through their actions that the New Testament was completed. Even now the name of Jesus is being preached to the uttermost parts of the earth. When the Holy Spirit came, the disciples received power from on high, as Jesus had said would happen.

After that the Holy Ghost Is Come upon You

Just before Jesus was crucified, a servant girl had said to Peter, "Thou also wast with Jesus of Galilee" but he had replied, "I know not this man of whom you speak." Then the cock crowed. It was then that Peter suddenly came to his senses and, realizing what he had done, he went out and wept bitterly. Jesus had already said that Peter would deny Him three times. When Peter realized that this is what he had done, he fell into deep despair. Imagine how he must have felt. He probably wanted to crawl into a hole and hide. He would not have known what to do with himself and probably thought that everyone knew what he had done.

But later, when the Holy Spirit came down upon Peter, his heart experienced a complete change. All the despair vanished from his heart and he cried out with a loud voice, "Ye . . . killed the Prince of life" Acts 3:14-15. "There is none other name under heaven given among men, whereby we must be saved . . . Whether it be right in the sight of God to hearken unto you more than unto God, judge ye" Acts 4:12, 19.

Whence had this tremendous courage arisen? The Holy Spirit had moved his heart. It is events such as this that have been recorded in the Bible and passed on down to us.

The disciples watched as Jesus ascended into heaven. They were left gazing intently into the skies as He was received out of their sight.

> "And when he had spoken these things, while they beheld, he was taken up; and a cloud received him out of their sight. And while they looked stedfastly toward heaven as he went up, behold, two men stood by them in white apparel; Which also said, Ye men of Galilee, why stand ye gazing up into heaven? this same Jesus, which is taken up from you into heaven, shall so come in like manner as ye have seen him go into heaven." Acts 1:9-11

Perhaps you know the hymn with the following words:

> We've a story to tell to the nations,
> That shall turn their hearts to the right,
> A story of truth and mercy,
> A story of peace and light,
> A story of peace and light.
> For the darkness shall turn to dawning,
> And the dawning to noonday bright,
> And Christ's great kingdom shall come on earth,
> The kingdom of love and light.[12]

Just before Jesus ascended into heaven, He said to His disciples, "Ye shall receive power, after that the Holy Ghost is come upon you." As we read through the book of Acts from the beginning, we find that the gospel first began to be preached in Jerusalem and then continued to spread further afield until it went even as far as Rome.

In the course of these events, we read how Stephen's preaching enraged the Jews. When Stephen had finished speaking, they all ran at him and stoned him to death. As they did so, there was a man standing by, giving the incident his full approval and guarding the robes that they had taken off in order that they might get a better throw.

This man was Saul, and he was named after the first king of Israel. Later, when he came to realize the truth of the gospel, he changed his name to Paul. At this time, however, he was a merciless young man, as cold as ice, and he considered it only right that Stephen should be stoned. He arrested and killed anyone he could find who believed in Jesus and he tried to force these believers to curse Jesus. But then one day, as he was on his way to Damascus, he saw a great light coming down from heaven and he fell to the ground. He had encountered Jesus. God called Saul in order to make use of this tremendous zeal that he had in His own work.

Who would have known that more than half the New Testament would be written through this man? Some tremendous words were written through him.

Surely the Lord Is in this Place

Just as Jesus, the Son of God, appeared to Paul, He also revealed Himself to Nathanael here in John chapter 1. Nathanael saw the One of whom Isaiah had written:

> "[T]he government shall be upon his shoulder: and his name shall be called Wonderful, Counsellor, The mighty God, The everlasting Father, The Prince of Peace." Isaiah 9:6

Isaiah also wrote:

> "Nevertheless the dimness shall not be such as was in her vexation, when at the first he lightly afflicted the land of Zebulun and the land of Naphtali, and afterward did more grievously afflict her by the way of the sea, beyond Jordan, in Galilee of the nations. The people that walked in darkness have seen a great light: they that dwell in the land of the shadow of death, upon them hath the light shined." Isaiah 9:1-2

This light shone on Philip, Peter, and Nathanael. Jesus, who was this light, appeared in the land of Galilee.

> "Jesus answered and said unto him, Because I said unto thee, I saw thee under the fig tree, believest thou? thou shalt see greater things than these. And he saith unto him, Verily, verily, I say unto you, Hereafter ye shall see heaven open, and the angels of God ascending and descending upon the Son of man." John 1:50-51

"Did you say that because you were surprised that I said I saw you under the fig tree?" This is what Jesus was saying.

"Hereafter ye shall see heaven open, and the angels of God ascending and descending upon the Son of man."

Nathanael had recognized Jesus as the King of Israel, but Jesus was explaining that He would return some day as the King of the kingdom of heaven.

Long ago, Jacob, one of the ancestors of the Jews was fleeing from the wrath of his brother, Esau, and one night he took a stone for his pillow and laid down to sleep. In his dream he saw a long ladder reaching from the ground where he slept, right up to heaven, and angels were ascending and descending on the ladder. This was an answer to him from God. Let's read the account of this episode in Genesis chapter 28.

"And Jacob went out from Beersheba, and went toward Haran. And he lighted upon a certain place, and tarried there all night, because the sun was set; and he took of the stones of that place, and put them for his pillows, and lay down in that place to sleep. And he dreamed, and behold a ladder set up on the earth, and the top of it reached to heaven: and behold the angels of God ascending and descending on it. And, behold, the Lord stood above it, and said, I am the Lord God of Abraham thy father, and the God of Isaac: the land whereon thou liest, to thee will I give it, and to thy seed; And thy seed shall be as the dust of the earth, and thou shalt spread abroad to the west, and to the east, and to the north, and to the south: and in thee and in thy seed shall all the families of the earth be blessed. And, behold, I am with thee, and will keep thee in all places whither thou goest, and will bring thee again into this land; for I will not leave thee, until I have done that which I have spoken to thee of. And Jacob awaked out of his sleep, and he said, Surely the Lord is in this place; and I knew it not. And he was afraid, and said, How dreadful is this place! this is none other but the house of God, and this is the gate of heaven. And Jacob rose up early in the morning, and took the stone that he had put for his pillows, and set it up for a pillar, and poured oil upon the top of it. And he called the name of that place Bethel: but the name of that city was called Luz at the first. And Jacob vowed a vow, saying, If God will be with me, and will keep me in this way that I go, and will give me bread to eat, and raiment to put on, So that I come again to my father's house in peace; then shall the Lord be my God: And this stone, which I have set for a pillar, shall be God's house: and of all that thou shalt give me I will surely give the tenth unto thee." Genesis 28:10-22

This was hundreds of years before the law of the Jews was written, at a time when the word "tithe"[13] was not even in use, and yet Jacob said, "This is none other but the house of God, and this is the gate of heaven," and he vowed that he would give to God one tenth of everything that he received.

He was good at bargaining with God, wasn't he? He made a transaction with God; he would accept God as his own God, if the stipulated requirements were met.

If we think about the words of the hymns that we sing, we find that there was also a time when we made a transaction with God. Perhaps you know the hymn that includes the words:

> 'Tis done the great transaction's done.
> I am my Lord's and He is mine.[14]

The day we come to believe in Jesus is the day on which this transaction takes place. This is the moment when our spirits become connected with God.

When Nathanael came to realize who Jesus was and said, "Thou art the Son of God; thou art the King of Israel," Jesus could already see Nathanael's whole life as it lay before him. So Jesus was able to say to him, "Ye shall see heaven open, and the angels of God ascending and descending upon the Son of man."

The time will come when we, too, will see these things. When Jesus ascended into heaven, two men in white asked the disciples why they were standing looking into the sky. When Jesus returns, will any of us be looking up into the sky? I don't think so, since the saved people will be taken up to Him so suddenly. When Jesus returns, the trumpet will sound, but there will not be time for us to look up and wonder whether or not we will be taken. There will be no time to wonder whether or not we have passed the test.

"When the trumpet of the Lord shall sound and time shall be no more."[15] When this happens, there will not be time to look up. When Jesus comes, we will suddenly be taken out of the world, leaving our clothes and shoes behind. When will this perfect salvation take place?

"Receiving the end of your faith, even the salvation of your souls."
1 Peter 1:9

This is what happens first, isn't it? So once our spirits have been saved, what remains to be accomplished? The salvation of our flesh. When we experience the salvation of our flesh, not only will we leave our clothes behind, we will not need any spectacles or gold teeth either. It will be a complete transformation. When that day of complete salvation arrives and Jesus suddenly returns, we will not need any high-heeled shoes. We will not need to skip meals in order to lose weight. We will have been perfected. Doesn't it feel good just to imagine what it will be like it?

> Jesus the very thought of Thee
> With sweetness fills my breast;
> But sweeter far Thy face to see,
> And in Thy presence rest.[16]

This is the hope with which and by which we live. This was the hope that Jesus gave to Nathanael.

> "[T]hou shalt see greater things than these. And he saith unto him, Verily, verily, I say unto you, Hereafter ye shall see heaven open, and the angels of God ascending and descending upon the Son of man."
>
> John 1:50-51

Is there any hope like this in the world? Is there anything that we can hope for from this world? Is there anything that we can expect from anyone else as we are living in this world? There is nothing at all, is there? You may try to put your hopes in something or someone, but it will only bring disappointment.

We race forward until that time when we stand before the Lord and experience the perfect salvation. Since Jesus has said, "Follow Me," all we have to do is follow Him. So we all need to read the Bible and see how Jesus lived and what sort of Man He was. And we need to ask ourselves how we put our trust in Him and by what hope we live our lives in this world.

> "But sanctify the Lord God in your hearts: and be ready always to give an answer to every man that asketh you a reason of the hope that is in you with meekness and fear."
>
> 1 Peter 3:15

We are always being asked about the hope that is in us. What hope do we have in this world? There is a hymn about this too:

> My hope is built on nothing less
> Than Jesus' blood and righteousness.
> I dare not trust the sweetest frame,
> But wholly lean on Jesus' name.
> On Christ the solid Rock I stand;
> All other ground is sinking sand,
> All other ground is sinking sand.[17]

What an amazingly stable Rock this is!

I once read in a book that in Israel there are areas full of dirt and sand, and if you are not careful and miss your step, the ground beneath your feet may give way and you fall into a pit below. In such places, rocks play an extremely important role. If you step carefully on the rocks, you will not fall into any of the pits.

It is really important for each of us to re-examine our faith in Jesus. Everything in this world decays and vanishes, so there is no greater blessing than to hope and trust in the solid Rock of Jesus Christ.

6

The Wedding to Which Jesus Was Invited

John 2:1-11

The lack of wine at this wedding feast signifies the fact that the things of God have been snatched away from the life of man.
Even when two people marry and form a family, something is still lacking in their lives.
Jesus was the Person responsible for this wine, and His position was such that the wine had to pour forth from Him.
The blood of Jesus, this truly old and mature wine, was a part of God's plan from the moment that Adam sinned, and even before that time, and when Jesus shed His blood, the way was opened for all of mankind to be able to be saved.

John 2:1-11

[1] And the third day there was a marriage in Cana of Galilee; and the mother of Jesus was there: [2] And both Jesus was called, and his disciples, to the marriage. [3] And when they wanted wine, the mother of Jesus saith unto him, They have no wine.

[4] Jesus saith unto her, Woman, what have I to do with thee? mine hour is not yet come.

[5] His mother saith unto the servants, Whatsoever he saith unto you, do it.

[6] And there were set there six waterpots of stone, after the manner of the purifying of the Jews, containing two or three firkins apiece. [7] Jesus saith unto them, Fill the waterpots with water. And they filled them up to the brim. [8] And he saith unto them, Draw out now, and bear unto the governor of the feast. And they bare it. [9] When the ruler of the feast had tasted the water that was made wine, and knew not whence it was: (but the servants which drew the water knew;) the governor of the feast called the bridegroom,

[10] And saith unto him, Every man at the beginning doth set forth good wine; and when men have well drunk, then that which is worse: but thou hast kept the good wine until now.

[11] This beginning of miracles did Jesus in Cana of Galilee, and manifested forth his glory; and his disciples believed on him.

There Was a Wedding in Cana

The above passage describes a scene at a wedding, a typical event that could take place in any household. Weddings have taken place throughout history. Such marriages have resulted in our being born and living in this world, and this is the way in which history will continue. During this particular wedding, however, a completely unexpected event occurred. Through this incident, we can examine how God began His work in the world of man.

There is a rather strange element to this episode. The mother of Jesus was invited to this wedding feast, as were Jesus and His disciples. The identity of the bride and groom, however, is not revealed; instead we are presented with a story about wine. Usually, when talking about a wedding, the first information to be passed on is the names of the bride and groom, and then mention is generally made about the guests. Strange to say, however, the story on this occasion centers on a matter involving the guests, the servants, and the ruler of the feast.

At this wedding feast, the wine, the element that would have contributed most to the festive mood of the party, was running out. Doesn't there appear to be a deeper meaning to be found within this passage? They had run out of wine at a seemingly ordinary wedding and so Jesus made some for them. Wine is not the kind of drink that can be made in an instant by mixing water with some other ingredients. These days there may be scientific methods that can be used to produce wine very quickly, but two thousand years ago the grapes had to be pressed and the juice allowed to ferment and mature before it became wine. At this wedding feast, however, Jesus made the wine in an instant.

This was the first miracle that Jesus performed. In certain respects, He might come across as some kind of magician here, but this was actually a miracle of tremendous consequence.

> "And the third day there was a marriage in Cana of Galilee; and the mother of Jesus was there."
>
> John 2:1

As I am reading the Bible, whenever I come across expressions that refer to a number of day, such as, "on the third day," or "after two days," I pay close attention. The term, "the third day," has a very profound connection with Jesus.

On one occasion, Jesus said, "I cast out devils, and I do cures today and tomorrow, and the third day I shall be perfected" Luke 13:32. Also, Moses, when negotiating with the pharaoh for the release of the Israelites, asked that they be permitted to go a three-day journey into the wilderness and there offer a sacrifice to the Lord. He argued with the pharaoh, insisting that a three-day journey was necessary.[1] The term, "three days," is also connected with Jesus' resurrection.

Why, then, did this incident also take place "on the third day"? We are also told that, Mary, the mother of Jesus, was invited to this wedding. It appears that she too had an important role to play at this wedding feast.

> "And both Jesus was called, and his disciples, to the marriage."
>
> John 2:2

A wedding feast is not just open to anyone. With the exception perhaps of beggars, only those with invitations may attend. Jesus and His disciples were invited to this wedding.

The Wine Gave Out

> "And when they wanted wine, the mother of Jesus saith unto him, They have no wine."
>
> John 2:3

Well into the proceedings, the wine, the most important element of the feast, came very close to running out.

So the mother of Jesus said to Him, "They have no wine."

Take a look now at how Jesus replied.

"Woman, what have I to do with thee? mine hour is not yet come."
John 2:4

It would be very easy to misunderstand these words. An answer like this could upset any mother and it would be considered extremely impudent no matter where you were in the world. Suppose, for example, a mother told her child to do something and the child retorted, "Woman, what do I have to do with you?" Would the father just ignore it? He would probably say something like:

"How dare you talk to your mother like that?"

The child would probably get a severe reprimand.

Nowhere in John chapter 2 does it say, however, that Jesus' reply vexed or upset Mary. She just heard His words. But why did Jesus say this?

"Jesus saith unto her, Woman, what have I to do with thee? mine hour is not yet come."
John 2:4

This indicates that there was an hour for Jesus, but that hour had not yet come. There is also an hour, or a time, for everyone born within the history of mankind. There is a time to be born and a time to die.[2] Jesus' hour, however, was completely different from that of anyone else.

Then Jesus' mother spoke again:

"His mother saith unto the servants, Whatsoever he saith unto you, do it."
John 2:5

Even though Mary was Jesus' mother, it appears that she acknowledged the absolute authority of her Son and she told the servants to do whatever He said.

How important was this wine to warrant Jesus' making some new wine such a great event? Let's think about this. For the Jews, wine was the most important alcoholic beverage. If the wine were to run out at a gathering, the festive atmosphere would be destroyed.

In the Bible, however, wine always offers some explanation of Jesus' blood. This is particularly true in the Gospels of Matthew, Mark, and Luke.

> "And he took the cup, and gave thanks, and gave it to them, saying, Drink ye all of it; For this is my blood of the new testament, which is shed for many for the remission of sins. But I say unto you, I will not drink henceforth of this fruit of the vine, until that day when I drink it new with you in my Father's kingdom."   Matthew 26:27-29

Jesus said of the wine, "[T]his is my blood."

Perhaps it was to explain Jesus' blood in advance that we are presented with this scene at the wedding in John chapter 2. We should see this incident as being quite different from an ordinary wedding at which they happened to run out of wine. Only then can we make the connection between Mary's request and Jesus' words, "Woman, what have I to do with thee?"

This mother, Jesus' mother, did not listen to these words as an ordinary mother would listen to her son. The wine here, too, has a very different significance to the wine that is served at any other wedding feast to contribute to the gaiety of the atmosphere. Jesus was the Person responsible for this wine, and His position was such that the wine had to pour forth from Him.

So it was that when Mary told Jesus that the wine at the wedding feast had run out, He said to her, "Woman, what have I to do with thee?"

Mary's action here is also interesting. If the wine had run out, surely she should have turned to whoever was responsible for supplying the wine in the first place. Why did she turn to her Son for help? He was not a wine merchant or the owner of a winery, so why did she say to her Son, "They have no wine"? Actually, they were just running out of wine, but she said that they had no wine at all.

Woman, What Have I to Do with Thee?

Let's read John chapter 2 verses 3 and 4 one more time.

> "And when they wanted wine, the mother of Jesus saith unto him, They have no wine. Jesus saith unto her, Woman, what have I to do with thee? mine hour is not yet come."

Here, when Jesus heard His mother say that they had no wine, He knew that this was true. Why was there no wine? It was in order that an extremely important point might be explained that the wine ran out at this wedding feast. As the young couple set out on their life together at this wedding feast, at this place where a new family was being formed, Mary was not speaking from the position of Jesus' mother, but rather in that of a woman.

As we consider this wedding feast, we also need to take into account an event that took place at the very beginning of the history of mankind. There was something that happened at that time that made it inevitable that Jesus should answer His mother with these words, "Woman, what have I to do with thee?" This is because it was at that time that a woman brought about this lack of wine.

127

The incident occurred long ago when Adam's wife, Eve, forfeited the life that she had been able to enjoy as a human being with whom God was well pleased. God had told Adam, "Of every tree of the garden thou mayest freely eat; but of the tree of the knowledge of good and evil, thou shalt not eat of it" Genesis 2:16-17. Then one day, the serpent approached Eve. Let's turn to Genesis and read what happened.

> "Now the serpent was more subtil than any beast of the field which the Lord God had made. And he said unto the woman, Yea, hath God said, Ye shall not eat of every tree of the garden? And the woman said unto the serpent, We may eat of the fruit of the trees of the garden: But of the fruit of the tree which is in the midst of the garden, God hath said, Ye shall not eat of it, neither shall ye touch it, lest ye die. And the serpent said unto the woman, Ye shall not surely die: For God doth know that in the day ye eat thereof, then your eyes shall be opened, and ye shall be as gods, knowing good and evil. And when the woman saw that the tree was good for food, and that it was pleasant to the eyes, and a tree to be desired to make one wise, she took of the fruit thereof, and did eat, and gave also unto her husband with her; and he did eat. And the eyes of them both were opened, and they knew that they were naked; and they sewed fig leaves together, and made themselves aprons." Genesis 3:1-7

In the course of their conversation, the serpent tricked Eve into saying of the forbidden fruit, "God hath said, Ye shall not eat of it, neither shall ye touch it, lest ye die." God had actually said, "In the day that thou eatest thereof thou shalt surely die," but Eve quoted Him as having said, "Lest ye die." She doubted God's words and in the end she ate from the fruit of the tree of the knowledge of good and evil.

In this way, the woman, Eve, opened the first door through which sin might enter this world. First she ate some of the fruit and then she gave some to her husband to eat, thus leaving the path wide open for sin to enter in. This woman took the lead, opening the path for sin to enter.

What answer should Eve have given to the serpent? When the serpent asked, "Yea, hath God said, Ye shall not eat of every tree of the garden?" she should have answered, "What has that got to do with me?" When God commanded that the fruit of the tree of the knowledge of good and evil was not to be eaten, had He summoned both Adam and Eve in order to say this? Or did He address these words to Adam alone? He gave this command to Adam alone. He did not say a word of this to Eve.

> "And the Lord God took the man, and put him into the garden of Eden to dress it and to keep it. And the Lord God commanded the man, saying, Of every tree of the garden thou mayest freely eat: But of the tree of the knowledge of good and evil, thou shalt not eat of it: for in the day that thou eatest thereof thou shalt surely die."
> Genesis 2:15-17

The word "thou" means "you" in the singular form. Eve did not even hear these words. God gave this command to Adam alone. In Genesis chapter 3 verse 1 it says:

> "Now the serpent was more subtil than any beast of the field which the Lord God had made. And he said unto the woman, Yea, hath God said, Ye shall not eat of every tree of the garden?"

The word "ye" means "you" in the plural form. The serpent said, "Hath God said, Ye shall not eat?" This is precisely the problem. Eve should have said to the serpent something like, "Why are you including me?" But what did she say?

> "And the woman said unto the serpent, We may eat of the fruit of the trees of the garden."
> Genesis 3:2

129

God had definitely been addressing Adam when He said, "Of the tree of the knowledge of good and evil, thou shalt not eat of it." But the snake crept along to Eve and carefully twisted these words, saying:

"Yea, hath God said, Ye shall not eat of every tree of the garden?"

The word "ye" entered Eve's ears and so how did she answer? She answered using the word "we."

If Eve had only thought for a moment, she might have said:

"Why are you dragging me into this? I don't know anything about it. Go and ask my husband."

That is all she needed to have said, but she included herself and answered:

"We may eat."

The seed that the serpent had planted was already growing.

When the woman, Jesus' mother, came and spoke with Him at this wedding feast at Cana, the voice of Eve echoed behind the scenes, the voice of the woman who many years earlier should have said, "If we eat from the tree of the knowledge of good and evil, we will surely die." Now this woman at the wedding feast came to say something that was quite different from the words that Eve had spoken.

> "And when they wanted wine, the mother of Jesus saith unto him, They have no wine."   John 2:3

She said that they had no wine. Jesus' answer to this was completely unexpected:

"Woman, what have I to do with thee?"

These words bear some reference to the relationship between the first man, Adam, and the woman, Eve.

If Eve had said clearly, "What does that have to do with me? That's Adam's responsibility," things would have turned out very differently. Instead, as this woman, one of the original progenitors of the human race, made the big mistake of receiving sin into this world, she took a great responsibility upon herself. And now, Mary was also taking on a certain responsibility when she spoke to Jesus about the wine. At this time, Jesus answered her, saying, "Woman, what have I to do with thee? Mine hour is not yet come," but actually from the content here, we can see that He definitely had something to do with the wine. As He said to her:

"Woman, what have I to do with thee?"

He was saying that this was not a matter in which a woman could be involved. Jesus' time would come and no one could be involved in the work that He was to carry out through His death on the cross. No one on earth could possibly help in, or contribute anything to, Jesus' death; this was work that God alone could accomplish.

At this wedding at Cana we witness the second woman making amends where the first woman had failed. It was the responsibility of the second woman to store God's word in her heart.

"Woman, what have I to do with thee? Mine hour is not yet come."

When Jesus said this to Mary, it was not for her to take the initiative as the first woman, Eve, had done; Mary had to remain silent. This was not a matter for her to try to deal with on impulse. It was reasonable that she should address the lack of actual physical wine, but when it came to the matter of the true wine and Jesus Himself having to be completely broken, it was not for her to say anything.

> "For Adam was first formed, then Eve. And Adam was not deceived, but the woman being deceived was in the transgression. Notwithstanding she shall be saved in childbearing, if they continue in faith and charity and holiness with sobriety." 1 Timothy 2:13-15

Who, according to this passage, was first deceived? It was Eve, wasn't it? When this woman Mary spoke with Jesus, they were each talking about completely and fundamentally different matters. Mary, therefore, reflected quietly and deeply on Jesus' words. She was coming to realize her position and how God had used her body in the process of carrying out His work and bringing His Son, Jesus into the world.

The Power of the Highest Shall Overshadow Thee

Mary was a woman who was devoted to God's word. She was to be married and some day start a family, but suddenly something completely unexpected happened to her. She was engaged to a young man by the name of Joseph and the day of their wedding was fast approaching, but then suddenly one day, quite out of the blue, an angel appeared to her. The angel addressed her with the words, "Hail, thou that art highly favoured." She must have been really startled. This woman was about to be married. She was supposed to be preparing herself for her husband and full of all the female virtues, but now, suddenly, an angel appeared to her, telling her things that she would never have thought of in her wildest dreams. She was deeply shocked. Imagine how she must have felt. What would have become of a woman who was found to be pregnant while she was engaged to be married? If her fiancé had nothing to do with the pregnancy, do you think the wedding would still take place?

> "And in the sixth month the angel Gabriel was sent from God unto a city of Galilee, named Nazareth, To a virgin espoused to a man whose name was Joseph, of the house of David; and the virgin's name was Mary. And the angel came in unto her, and said, Hail, thou that art highly favoured, the Lord is with thee: blessed art thou among women. And when she saw him, she was troubled at his saying, and cast in her mind what manner of salutation this should be."
>
> Luke 1:26-29

The angel appeared to her and offered her what would have seemed to be a greeting so completely absurd that she could not help but wonder what this all meant.

> "And the angel said unto her, Fear not, Mary: for thou hast found favour with God."
>
> Luke 1:30

The words of the angel continued to be astonishing.

> "And, behold, thou shalt conceive in thy womb, and bring forth a son, and shalt call his name JESUS."
>
> Luke 1:31

First, the angel addressed her as being "highly favoured" and then he told her she would conceive in her womb. This meant not only her own ruin, but also that of her whole family.

> "He shall be great, and shall be called the Son of the Highest: and the Lord God shall give unto him the throne of his father David: And he shall reign over the house of Jacob for ever; and of his kingdom there shall be no end."
>
> Luke 1:32-33

The angel told Mary that she would give birth to a great Person; through her the Son of God was to be born.

> "Then said Mary unto the angel, How shall this be, seeing I know not a man? And the angel answered and said unto her, The Holy Ghost shall come upon thee, and the power of the Highest shall overshadow thee: therefore also that holy thing which shall be born of thee shall

be called the Son of God. And, behold, thy cousin Elisabeth, she hath also conceived a son in her old age: and this is the sixth month with her, who was called barren. For with God nothing shall be impossible. And Mary said, Behold the handmaid of the Lord; be it unto me according to thy word. And the angel departed from her."

Luke 1:34-38

When the angel said that Mary would conceive, she said, "How shall this be, seeing I know not a man?" It was not that she did not know Joseph; she meant that she had not had any sexual contact with a man. She spoke frankly. Then the angel told her the amazing news. Mary accepted the words of the angel and kept them in her heart. As the angel said, "For with God nothing shall be impossible," Mary stored up these words in her heart, and everything happened as the angel said.

A Virgin Shall Conceive and Bear a Son

As we read through the Bible, we come across certain points that appear to be somewhat strange. One example of this is to be found in the genealogy of Jesus in the first chapter of Matthew's Gospel. The chapter begins:

> "The book of the generation of Jesus Christ, the son of David, the son of Abraham. Abraham begat Isaac; and Isaac begat Jacob; and Jacob begat Judas and his brethren; And Judas begat Phares and Zara of Thamar; and Phares begat Esrom; and Esrom begat Aram; And Aram begat Aminadab; and Aminadab begat Naasson; and Naasson begat Salmon; And Salmon begat Booz of Rachab; and Booz begat Obed of Ruth; and Obed begat Jesse; And Jesse begat David the king."
>
> Matthew 1:1-6

Here we have a long list of who was born to whom, and probably few people give it a second thought. An uninterrupted genealogy is recorded here, telling us who was born to which man, and, occasionally, through which woman. In each case, it says that the man begot the child.

There is an old Korean poem that includes the lines:

> My father gave me birth
> But my mother raised me.

It was not until I had grown to be a man that I really understood what this meant. Even today when a child misbehaves, people may wonder who his father is. We also use the expression, "Like father, like son."

When we read right through to the end of this genealogy of Jesus, however, what do we find? It says, "Mary, of whom was born Jesus."

"And Jacob begat Joseph the husband of Mary, of whom was born Jesus, who is called Christ." Matthew 1:16

To whom does it say that Jesus was born? It says that He was born to the woman Mary.

"Now the birth of Jesus Christ was on this wise: When as his mother Mary was espoused to Joseph, before they came together, she was found with child of the Holy Ghost. Then Joseph her husband, being a just man, and not willing to make her a publick example, was minded to put her away privily. But while he thought on these things, behold, the angel of the Lord appeared unto him in a dream, saying, Joseph, thou son of David, fear not to take unto thee Mary thy wife: for that which is conceived in her is of the Holy Ghost. And she shall bring forth a son, and thou shalt call his name JESUS: for he shall save his people from their sins. Now all this was done, that it might be fulfilled which was spoken of the Lord by the prophet, saying: "Behold, a virgin shall be with child, and shall bring forth a son, and they shall call his name Emmanuel, which being interpreted is, God with us." Matthew 1:18-23

The angel of the Lord explained to Joseph the words of the prophet Isaiah:

"Therefore the Lord himself shall give you a sign; Behold, a virgin shall conceive, and bear a son, and shall call his name Immanuel."

Isaiah 7:14

Joseph must have been deeply disturbed to find that his beloved fiancée was pregnant. He was supposed to be marrying her, but now she was with child. It seems, however, that Joseph was very calm and levelheaded. He planned to break off the engagement quietly, knowing that if he told anyone about Mary's condition, she would be stoned to death. This was the way in which the Jews dealt with anyone found to have committed such an offense. In the book of Deuteronomy it says, "If a damsel that is a virgin be betrothed unto an husband, and a man find her in the city, and lie with her; Then ye shall bring them both out unto the gate of that city, and ye shall stone them with stones that they die" Deuteronomy 22:23-24.

Just as Joseph was thinking about putting Mary away secretly, however, an angel appeared to him in a dream and said, "Joseph, thou son of David, fear not to take unto thee Mary thy wife: for that which is conceived in her is of the Holy Ghost. And she shall bring forth a son, and thou shalt call his name Jesus" Matthew 1:20-21.

Joseph listened to the words of the angel and he and Mary were married. Later the two of them went to Bethlehem in order to register there for a census. Their journey to Bethlehem was far from ordinary; there was a purpose, a plan, and a meaning behind it, and its timing was also of significance. It was an arduous process, and in the midst of it, Jesus, the Son of God, was born in Bethlehem.

Whatsoever He Saith unto You, Do It

Mary had physically given birth to Jesus, but she did not have any authority over Him. At this wedding feast Mary heard the words which, as a woman, she needed to hear. Jesus said to her:

"Woman, what have I to do with thee?" John 2:4

When Mary heard this, she probably thought of the words the angel had spoken to her long before, telling her that she would bear a Child who would be the Son of God. So she accepted Jesus' words without any protest. In her heart she had believed everything that the angel had told her and she had said, "Be it unto me according to thy word" Luke 1:38. This was also the case here at the wedding feast. The words she addressed to the servants reflected what was in her heart.

"Jesus saith unto her, Woman, what have I to do with thee? mine hour is not yet come. His mother saith unto the servants, Whatsoever he saith unto you, do it." John 2:4-5

When Jesus said, "Woman, what have I to do with thee?" this woman accepted these words in her heart as the words of God. Mary knew that these were no ordinary words and she listened to them with the purity of heart of a person who keeps the words of God in her heart. So, even though this was her Son, she told the servants, "Whatsoever he saith unto you, do it."

Come unto Me, and Drink

There is one point we need to consider here before we continue. The lack of wine at this wedding feast signifies the fact that the things of God have been snatched away from the life of man. It is revealed here, that the word of God has been stolen away from man's life. Even when two people marry and form a family, something is still lacking in their lives.

I sometimes try to imagine the grief that Adam and Eve must have felt when they were driven out of the Garden of Eden and had to go far away. When two people truly love one another, you would imagine it would not matter to them where they went or what their circumstances were as long as they were together and their love did not change. Where there is true love, you would imagine that nothing else would matter.

At that time, however, Adam and Eve lost something that made their whole situation very different. In this new family that was just beginning and full of the love of this young couple, it was of no concern to Adam and Eve if they had no house to live in. Their grief was not over the loss of any of the mundane things of life; there was something else that they had lost. What a wretched situation man would be in if all he had was his life in this world.

Consequently, even though the descendants of this couple who were driven out of the Garden of Eden marry and begin new families, their lives are always empty like the six waterpots and there is nothing they can do about it. Man is always thirsting after something to fill this emptiness and he can never rid himself of this thirst.

There is a hymn that expresses the only solution to this thirst that man has:

> Fly as a bird to your mountain
> Thou who art weary of sin;
> Go to the clear flowing fountain
> Where you may wash and be clean.[3]

This is what Jesus was referring to when He cried out in John's Gospel chapter 7:

> "In the last day, that great day of the feast, Jesus stood and cried, saying, If any man thirst, let him come unto me, and drink. He that believeth on me, as the scripture hath said, out of his belly shall flow rivers of living water. (But this spake he of the Spirit, which they that believe on him should receive: for the Holy Ghost was not yet given; because that Jesus was not yet glorified.)" John 7:37-39

Even though this newly-formed family would have been overflowing with joy at the wedding feast, there was still something missing. Their lives were not connected with God's plan. If the Holy Spirit of God is not Lord of the household, even though its members may live and eat well, that will be the extent of their lives. They will merely live as human beings.

The family that was starting out at the time of this wedding needed the blood that Jesus Christ would shed once for all at His holy death, and this would have nothing to do with any woman. He had to go through the pain and suffering of that death. Only then would the Holy Spirit come to man. This was what was missing and what this family needed.

The Precious Blood that the Lord Shed for Me

What is the significance of Jesus appearing in the flesh and His changing the water into wine? If we take another look at the passage from John chapter 7 quoted above, we can see that the Holy Spirit had not yet been given. The prime factor was missing. As the feast drew to an end, on the last day, the great day of the feast, the people were feeling empty. At that time the people who heard Jesus as He cried out, "If any man thirst, let him come unto me, and drink," were in the same thirsty state as the people at the wedding feast as the wine ran out.

>Jesus the Lord has shed His precious
>Blood on the cross.
>His blood has purified my spirit.
>He saved me from my sin.
>Jesus brought me sweet salvation
>From the clutch of sin.
>I now believe and I am standing
>Firm on the word of God.
>
>Jesus has died and shed His priceless
>Blood for my sake.
>He washed the sins that stained my spirit.
>Jesus has made me clean.
>Jesus brought me sweet salvation
>From the clutch of sin.
>I now believe and I am standing
>Firm on the word of God.
>
>My heart has known the love and kindness
>Christ gave to me.
>Now I have strength against temptation.
>He gives me strength to win.
>Jesus brought me sweet salvation
>From the clutch of sin.
>I now believe and I am standing
>Firm on the word of God.
>
>Jesus will keep me safe wherever
>Love leads me on.
>He guides me to His peaceful dwelling.
>He gives me perfect rest.
>Jesus brought me sweet salvation
>From the clutch of sin.

The Wedding to Which Jesus was Invited

> I now believe and I am standing
> Firm on the word of God.
>
> I do not trust in things I see, but
> In faith alone
> Walking the road with my Lord Jesus,
> Now I have found true joy.
> Jesus brought me sweet salvation
> From the clutch of sin.
> I now believe and I am standing
> Firm on the word of God.[4]

When I sing this hymn, I think to myself, "That is so true! That's really how it is!" These words are set to the music of the American song, Swanee River:

> Way down upon the Swanee River
> Far, far away,
> There's where my heart is turning ever,
> There's where the old folks stay.[5]

There is a huge difference between the words of the original song and those of this hymn.

> Jesus the Lord has shed His precious
> Blood on the cross.

What wonderful words these are! The feeling of peace that we experience in our hearts when the Holy Spirit takes control was what was needed in this family at the wedding in Cana. When the wine flowed, the guests were content, but their cheerful spirits were in danger of dying down as the wine ran out. When Jesus provided an abundance of new wine for the party, however, it brought with it a new joy for the guests to embrace. In the same way, we need to be soaked in the wine that quenches our spiritual thirst.

Another verse in the above hymn begins with the line:

> I do not trust in things I see, but
> In faith alone.

Even though we cannot see God, we believe in Him. Jesus Himself said, "Blessed are they that have not seen, and yet have believed" John 20:29.

If Any Man Thirst, Let Him Come unto Me, and Drink

> "And there were set there six waterpots of stone, after the manner of the purifying of the Jews, containing two or three firkins apiece."
> John 2:6

It was the custom amongst the Jews to draw water and wash themselves before attending any kind of ceremony. Here, too, there were six stone waterpots that were used for such ceremonial washing. There was a significance to there being six of these waterpots. In the Bible, the number "6" represents man and signifies that something is lacking. Jesus told them to fill these six stone waterpots to the brim.

> "Jesus saith unto them, Fill the waterpots with water. And they filled them up to the brim. And he saith unto them, Draw out now, and bear unto the governor of the feast. And they bare it." John 2:7-8

After they had filled the six stone waterpots to the brim, Jesus told them to draw some of the water from the pots and take it to the ruler of the feast. It seems that the servants were uncomplicated and simple-hearted. If I had been there, I am sure I would have tasted the liquid before taking it to the ruler of the feast, to avoid the possibility of an embarrassing situation. How could they just put water in the pots and draw from this as though it were wine? This could have gotten them into big trouble. It would have been a

The Wedding to Which Jesus was Invited

different matter if they had filled the pots with wine and then drawn from them, but they filled them with water and drew from them. Isn't this rather strange? But these servants were people who did as they were told.

> "When the ruler of the feast had tasted the water that was made wine, and knew not whence it was: (but the servants which drew the water knew;) the governor of the feast called the bridegroom, And saith unto him, Every man at the beginning doth set forth good wine; and when men have well drunk, then that which is worse: but thou hast kept the good wine until now."
>
> John 2:9-10

The ruler of the feast was the first to taste the wine and he declared that it was very tasty. The older a wine is, the tastier it becomes, and the oldest wines can be extremely expensive. I am told that some wines even run into thousands of dollars. This is why the date of production is always written on the label of a bottle of wine. A wine that is about thirty years old may not be cheap, but one that has been allowed to mature for a hundred years or more will be extremely expensive. Since the ruler of the feast said that the wine was so good, we can presume that he had tasted a very old wine.

So the ruler of the feast summoned the bridegroom and said, "You have kept the really good wine until last." "People usually serve the best wine first, and the worse wine later, but you have been serving good wine from start to finish." This is what he was saying. He praised the bridegroom in this way, and probably the bridegroom was also very surprised since he had no idea where this wine had come from. When the ruler of the feast said to the bridegroom, "Thou hast kept the good wine until now," it meant that this was the older, more mature wine. In Luke chapter 5 verse 39 it says, "No man also having drunk old wine straightway desireth new: for he saith, The old is better." A person who says, "The old wine is better," knows the true value of the old wine.

The Bible says that the ruler of the feast did not know where the wine had come from. This is true, since Jesus had made this wine. But the servants knew because they had obeyed Jesus' words without question. What does this tell us? Let's take a look at some of the words that God proclaimed continually through the prophet Isaiah:

> "Ho, every one that thirsteth, come ye to the waters, and he that hath no money; come ye, buy, and eat; yea, come, buy wine and milk without money and without price. Wherefore do ye spend money for that which is not bread? and your labour for that which satisfieth not? hearken diligently unto me, and eat ye that which is good, and let your soul delight itself in fatness. Incline your ear, and come unto me: hear, and your soul shall live; and I will make an everlasting covenant with you, even the sure mercies of David. Behold, I have given him for a witness to the people, a leader and commander to the people."
>
> Isaiah 55:1-4

This is Jesus, isn't it? Let's take another look at the first verse here. It says, "Ho, every one that thirsteth, come ye to the waters, and he that hath no money; come ye, buy, and eat; yea, come, buy wine and milk without money and without price." It says to buy wine, but there is no need to pay any money for it. Did the people at the wedding in Cana collect some money and go out and buy some wine? They did not, did they? This scene in which Jesus turned the water into wine is telling us that when anyone living in the world today truly believes in Jesus, he will be guided by the Holy Spirit.

> "This beginning of miracles did Jesus in Cana of Galilee, and manifested forth his glory; and his disciples believed on him."
>
> John 2:11

After Adam sinned, God said to the serpent, "The Seed of the woman will bruise your head." This was a prophecy, indicating that some day Jesus would have to come into this world and die on the cross.

> "And he said unto them, These are the words which I spake unto you, while I was yet with you, that all things must be fulfilled, which were written in the law of Moses, and in the prophets, and in the psalms, concerning me. Then opened he their understanding, that they might understand the scriptures." Luke 24:44-45

The blood of Jesus, this truly old and mature wine, was a part of God's plan from the moment that Adam sinned, and even before that time, and when Jesus shed His blood, the way was opened for all of mankind to be able to be saved. So it is that we often find references in the Bible to a direct relationship between Adam and Jesus, as, for example, in this verse from the letter to the Romans:

> "Wherefore, as by one man sin entered into the world, and death by sin; and so death passed upon all men, for that all have sinned." Romans 5:12

Let's also take a look at Romans chapter 5 from verse 17 to verse 19.

> "For if by one man's offence death reigned by one; much more they which receive abundance of grace and of the gift of righteousness shall reign in life by one, Jesus Christ.) Therefore as by the offence of one judgment came upon all men to condemnation; even so by the righteousness of one the free gift came upon all men unto justification of life. For as by one man's disobedience many were made sinners, so by the obedience of one shall many be made righteous."

It says here that through the disobedience of one man, Adam, sin entered into the world, and through the obedience of One, all of mankind were made righteous. Let's think about this. In what way was Jesus obedient?

Not As I Will

"O my Father, if it be possible, let this cup pass from me: nevertheless not as I will, but as thou wilt."　　　　　　　　　　Matthew 26:39[6]

When Jesus said here, "Not as I will," He was asking that events not turn out according to the will of His flesh. At this point, Jesus was experiencing tremendous anguish, and yet He said, "Not as I will, but as thou wilt." He was asking God to give Him the strength to let the Old Testament prophecies be fulfilled in Him since He was to die as it had been foretold. He had to die according to the scenario recorded in the Old Testament Scriptures, rise from the dead three days later, and ascend into heaven. After that, the Holy Spirit would come, and only then would faith arise within the hearts of men and only then would people come to know and appreciate the true value of this wine.

The miracle at this wedding feast provides a very good metaphor to demonstrate the overflowing love that we receive from God. Jesus used this one family as a setting in which to explain clearly this overflowing wine. This miracle at the wedding feast at Cana in Galilee when Jesus turned the water into wine serves to indicate the connection between Jesus and all the prophecies and promises that God made through the prophets in the Old Testament. We can see how these prophecies were fulfilled in Jesus' death on the cross and His subsequent resurrection three days later.

In other words, this incident show us that man is able to enjoy happiness through the intervention of God's work in the world of mankind. The Bible is also telling us that a new covenant came into effect through Jesus' obedience to all the prophecies recorded in the Old Testament. The original wine ran out and the new wine began to flow, but the two were not unrelated. This incident represents the moment when the prophecies and promises that God had made in advance were accomplished in Jesus.

When Jesus came to this wedding and turned the water into wine, He was not performing some kind of magic trick; He did this to demonstrate in advance the suffering and death that awaited Him. In other words, He was offering this as a form of warranty. He definitely was not acting in response to his mother Mary's words when she said, "They have no wine."

Jesus changed the water into wine at this wedding feast to show that He would accept the responsibility of fulfilling God's holy will through His own body. As Jesus made the wine in this way, He was explaining the deeply significant death that He would undergo.

As we continue to study John's Gospel, we will probably have the opportunity to take a look at just how terrible, painful, and grievous His death was.

7

Jesus and the Temple

John 2:12-25

The Jews had built a very impressive temple of gold and silver. But an even better temple, a more holy temple than had been hoped for by all the Jews put together, was being accomplished in Jesus Himself. It was because Jesus had to die and then rise again from the dead in order that this temple might be completed that He said, "Destroy this temple." This temple is the body of Jesus.

John 2:12-25

[12] After this he went down to Capernaum, he, and his mother, and his brethren, and his disciples: and they continued there not many days. [13] And the Jews' passover was at hand, and Jesus went up to Jerusalem,

[14] And found in the temple those that sold oxen and sheep and doves, and the changers of money sitting: [15] And when he had made a scourge of small cords, he drove them all out of the temple, and the sheep, and the oxen; and poured out the changers' money, and overthrew the tables; [16] And said unto them that sold doves, Take these things hence; make not my Father's house an house of merchandise.

[17] And his disciples remembered that it was written, The zeal of thine house hath eaten me up. [18] Then answered the Jews and said unto him, What sign shewest thou unto us, seeing that thou doest these things?

[19] Jesus answered and said unto them, Destroy this temple, and in three days I will raise it up.

[20] Then said the Jews, Forty and six years was this temple in building, and wilt thou rear it up in three days?

[21] But he spake of the temple of his body. [22] When therefore he was risen from the dead, his disciples remembered that he had said this unto them; and they believed the scripture, and the word which Jesus had said.

[23] Now when he was in Jerusalem at the passover, in the feast day, many believed in his name, when they saw the miracles which he did. [24] But Jesus did not commit himself unto them, because he knew all men, [25] And needed not that any should testify of man: for he knew what was in man.

He Went Down to Capernaum and Continued There Not Many Days

As we read through John's Gospel, it becomes evident that Jesus knew all about the nature and thoughts of people. Here, at the end of chapter 2, it says that Jesus knew all men and therefore did not commit Himself to anyone. The content of chapter 2 verse 12 is quite straightforward. It says:

> "After this he went down to Capernaum, he, and his mother, and his brethren, and his disciples: and they continued there not many days."

This verse is short and simple. Jesus went to Capernaum, but why did he only stay there a few days? Capernaum is often referred to in the other Gospels as well. It was a town in the region of Galilee. On one occasion, as Jesus was on His way to Galilee, He said, "No prophet is accepted in his own country." Luke 4:24 Jesus evangelized in this area more than in any other, and the disciples were also very active here. Even though Jesus carried out so much work here, the people there did not accept Him. Capernaum was one of the towns that Jesus mentioned in particular as He rebuked the area.

> "Then began he to upbraid the cities wherein most of his mighty works were done, because they repented not . . . And thou, Capernaum, which art exalted unto heaven, shalt be brought down to hell: for if the mighty works, which have been done in thee, had been done in Sodom, it would have remained until this day." Matthew 11:20, 23

It was just as it says in John chapter 1 verse 11:

> "He came unto his own, and his own received him not."

This was true of the Jewish nation as a whole, but it was also true of Capernaum where Jesus had concentrated so much of His effort. If you look carefully through the whole of the New Testament, you will find many such references.

The Passover of the Jews

"And the Jews' passover was at hand, and Jesus went up to Jerusalem."

John 2:13

Here we have reference to the Passover[1] of the Jews. This Passover of the Jews was a feast that was limited to the Jews alone. This is not the Passover spoken of by the Church in New Testament times after Jesus had died. In the New Testament it says that Christ is our Passover.[2] There is also a hymn that includes the lines,

> Sprinkle your soul with the blood of the Lamb
> And I will pass, will pass over you.[3]

Those who believe in Christ know that Jesus Christ who shed His blood and died on the cross, is the Passover Lamb. When the Holy Spirit came, many people came to realize this truth, and we too have come to believe it.

At the time of Jesus, however, even though He spoke about the Feast of the Passover, His disciples did not know what He was saying. All they knew was the Passover that appears in the Old Testament, from Exodus chapter 12.

The Israelites first observed the Passover when Moses led them out of Egypt, and God commanded them to keep this feast as an everlasting ordinance. When Pharaoh refused to release the Israelites, they insisted that they had to go a three-day journey into the wilderness and there offer sacrifices to God. Then, after their flight from Egypt, as they were wandering in the wilderness, God spoke to them through Moses and told them more regarding the Feast of the Passover. Consequently, from the time of that first Passover until Jesus came to this earth, during that long period of 1,400 years, the Israelites kept the Feast of the Passover wherever they went.

It is true that during their time of captivity in Babylon, the Israelites were not able to observe this feast, but once they had returned to their land, it was restored to some extent, and the temple was rebuilt, those who remained living in other countries would come to Jerusalem every year to observe the Feast of the Passover.

Our Passover Lamb

> "And the Jews' passover was at hand, and Jesus went up to Jerusalem."
>
> John 2:13

Jesus' steps toward Jerusalem were quite different from those of any journey that we might imagine. Jesus went up to Jerusalem once, and then He went again, and the third time He went He had to face His death there. This is indicated here when it says, "The Jews' passover was at hand, and Jesus went up to Jerusalem." This was Jesus' path to the suffering of the cross He was to bear, the path to His death. As Jesus went up to Jerusalem to observe the Feast of the Passover at this time, it was but the first step. The second step would bring Him closer to His death, and the third step would be the last. Thus, there is a very deep significance to the fact that Jesus went up to observe the Passover.

After Jesus had been crucified, had died, and had risen from the dead on the third day, He appeared to His disciples and said, "All things must be fulfilled, which were written in the law of Moses." Then He opened their minds to understand the Scriptures.[4] He explained to them how His own death corresponded to the Passover of the Jews.

At the time of the Passover, the Jews would come from various lands to the temple in Jerusalem. Around 600 years before Christ (606-586 BC), the Jews who had been taken as captives to Babylon, dispersed and settled in various countries in the region of the Middle East. Every year when it came time to observe the Feast of the Passover, these Jews would all gather in Jerusalem. Just as people nowadays return to their homes at the holiday season, the Jews would return to Jerusalem, the home of their hearts, their thoughts, and their spirits, and there they would offer sacrifices to God.

The term, "Passover," holds the meaning of passing over, in the sense of God's judgment passing over the Jews. All the animals that were slaughtered on the day of the Passover offer an explanation of the image of Jesus Christ.

> "Purge out therefore the old leaven, that ye may be a new lump, as ye are unleavened. For even Christ our passover is sacrificed for us."
>
> 1 Corinthians 5:7

It says here that Jesus is our Passover. There is a difference between "the Jews' passover" and "Christ our passover." Many animals had to die every year during the Passover of the Jews. Also, the temple was a necessary feature in the celebration of this feast. At first there was the tabernacle, then later the temple building was constructed.[5]

The sacrificial animals all served to explain the image of Jesus Christ. Bulls, calves, sheep, or pigeons would be sacrificed, each presenting a different side of Jesus' nature. The bull, going silently to the slaughter, presents an image of Christ who did not say a word as He was dragged to His death. When the Jews sacrificed a lamb, they were not to break any bone of it.[6] Neither were any of Jesus' bones broken when He was sacrificed.

Christ, who had no sin, died for us, who are sinners. As the Bible says, we are redeemed with the precious blood of Christ, as of a lamb without blemish and without spot.[7] The Jews were not permitted to use a lamb for sacrifice if it had anything wrong with it at all, whether it had a broken limb, or had been wounded, bitten or marred in any way. Since the lamb was to be "without blemish and without spot," it was not to have any speckles either. Speckles are hereditary, but Jesus Christ did not inherit anything from man. Jesus was not born through the lineage of man, but through the Holy Spirit of the eternal God. Therefore the Bible refers to Him as "a lamb without blemish and without spot."

The Lamb of God Which Taketh Away the Sin of the World

All the images of the Christ who was to come into the world and die converged on Jesus. Never had such an event taken place before in the history of mankind and never would it take place again. So as Jesus went up to Jerusalem for the last time, His walk was a death march; His feet were taking Him to the place where He would die.

Here in John chapter 2 it says that "the Jews' Passover was at hand" John 2:13. When the feast of the Passover came around, the Jews, who were waiting longingly for the coming of the Christ, performed the ceremonials of the feast in accordance with God's promise and commandments. This continuous annual Passover of the Jews, however, was only a shadow of a greater Passover to come, the Passover made complete with the sacrifice of Jesus. On the day of that sacrifice, a wooden plaque bearing an inscription of the charge brought against Him was attached to the cross above His head. It read:

"THE KING OF THE JEWS." Mark 15:26

"The King of the Jews." Jesus was not just an ordinary king—He was the Christ who died, taking upon Himself all the sins of the Jews.

The Bible tells us that on the day Jesus was crucified "the veil of the temple was rent in twain from the top to the bottom; and the earth did quake, and the rocks rent" Matthew 27:51. Many people realized at that time that Jesus was definitely a righteous Man. They only discovered this after they had crucified Him.

The tabernacle in the Old Testament was the place where the Israelites offered their sacrifices before the temple was built. It was lofty and made with curtains of blue, purple, and scarlet linen. Inside were the holy place and the most holy place, with a veil[8] separating the two. Seeking atonement for the sinners, the high priest would first cleanse himself. He would then go through the holy place and pass behind the veil to the most holy place where he would sprinkle the blood of the sacrificial animal before the ark of the covenant. The laws governing the offering of sacrifices were so strict that if a sinner went into the tabernacle and tried to enter the most holy place, he would die even before he had passed behind the veil.

All of these laws and ceremonies performed in the temple were merely a shadow of Jesus Christ. We might compare them to blueprints. A building is constructed according to the designs set out in the blueprints, all the details translating into physical attributes of the final construction. The blueprints may be small, but they are magnified in the construction work so that the building turns out much larger.

Let's consider once again the passage in John chapter 1 from verse 9 through verse 13:

> "That was the true Light, which lighteth every man that cometh into the world. He was in the world, and the world was made by him, and the world knew him not. He came unto his own, and his own received him not. But as many as received him, to them gave he power to become the sons of God, even to them that believe on his name: Which were born, not of blood, nor of the will of the flesh, nor of the will of man, but of God."

Here in verse 11 it says, "He came unto his own, and his own received him not." This refers to the Jews alone. Verse 12, however, where it says, "But as many as received him, to them gave he power to become the sons of God, even to them that believe on his name," applies to all who believe. As a nation, the Jews did not receive Jesus. They rejected Him and had Him crucified. Even after He rose from the dead and ascended into heaven, they opposed Him and so it was inevitable that they should be destined to be scattered throughout the world.

It was because Jesus' own people rejected Him that the apostles turned to the gentiles and spread the gospel amongst them.[9] Consequently, we too, as gentiles, have come to see Jesus through the New Testament and come to know that He is the true Son of God and the Lamb of God. Now we can find the Lamb of God. This was how John the Baptist described Him:

> "The next day John seeth Jesus coming unto him, and saith, Behold the Lamb of God, which taketh away the sin of the world." John 1:29

When it says here that He takes away the sin of the world, this clearly does not only apply to the sins of the Jews; it means the sin of everyone in the world.

Let's turn now to the very last book in the Old Testament, the book of Malachi.

> "Behold, I will send my messenger, and he shall prepare the way before me: and the Lord, whom ye seek, shall suddenly come to his temple, even the messenger of the covenant, whom ye delight in: behold, he shall come, saith the Lord of hosts. But who may abide the day of his coming? and who shall stand when he appeareth? for he is like a refiner's fire, and like fullers' soap." Malachi 3:1-2

This passage brings to mind the verse in John chapter 1 that tells of a man who "came for a witness, to bear witness of the Light" John 1:7. This man was John the Baptist.

> "Behold, I will send my messenger, and he shall prepare the way before me . . . saith the Lord of hosts."

John the Baptist was the messenger who came to prepare the way before the Lord.

> "[A]nd the Lord, whom ye seek, shall suddenly come to his temple."

Who is this Lord? It is Jesus Christ. Christ came to His temple, thus fulfilling these words that the prophet Malachi had recorded some four hundred years earlier.

> "[A]nd the Lord, whom ye seek, shall suddenly come to his temple, even the messenger of the covenant, whom ye delight in: behold, he shall come, saith the Lord of hosts. But who may abide the day of his coming? and who shall stand when he appeareth?"

Who is this talking about? As was foretold in the book of Malachi, a messenger came first to clear the way for Jesus. Then Jesus Himself came and carried out His work. John the Baptist is the one who prepared the way for the coming of the Christ, and Jesus is the One who appeared in His temple.

Jesus and the Temple

Make Not My Father's House an House of Merchandise.

> "And found in the temple those that sold oxen and sheep and doves, and the changers of money sitting: And when he had made a scourge of small cords, he drove them all out of the temple, and the sheep, and the oxen; and poured out the changers' money, and overthrew the tables."
>
> John 2:14-15

When Jesus entered the temple, His eyes met with quite a spectacle. People were selling all sorts of animals there—bulls, lambs, goats, pigeons. From one corner the priests were watching over the scene. In another corner, the moneychangers were conducting their business. The Jews who had come from other lands had brought with them the currency of those lands, and this could not be used in the temple so it had to be exchanged for holy money. The temple had its own unit of currency, and the moneychangers made quite a profit from their service. On top of all of this, the temple also collected site rental fees from the merchants.

This was supposed to be the temple of God, the place where God was worshipped, so the moment Jesus' eyes met with this scene, He was filled with rage. He made a whip of cords and with it proceeded to drive the animals out of the temple. He also overturned the tables of the moneychangers. Quite a commotion must have broken loose in the temple.

Nowhere in the Bible does it say that Jesus laughed or smiled. He must have come across as a very solemn person. Perhaps this was because of the death that lay ahead of Him. Nevertheless, this meek and gentle Man threw the temple into chaos. Imagine the scene as the coins of the moneychangers clattered across the marble floor of the temple and people rushed in all directions, diving after the money. Visiting Jews from other lands probably stood around in utter confusion, watching as animals ran from one corner to another trying to escape the whip.

When Jesus came to the sellers of doves, however, He simply said:

"Take these things away."

"And said unto them that sold doves, Take these things hence; make not my Father's house an house of merchandise." John 2:16

These people would not have made much money from selling these birds. Those who had enough money bought a lamb or a bull to offer as a sacrifice for their sins. The doves were sold to the poor who could barely afford to offer any kind of sacrifice. Clearly there was little profit to be made from this kind of sales. At times like this, it seems that Jesus felt great sympathy for the poor.

Let's turn now to the book of Leviticus.

"And if his oblation be a sacrifice of peace offering, if he offer it of the herd; whether it be a male or female, he shall offer it without blemish before the Lord." Leviticus 3:1

When the Israelites sacrificed a bull as a peace offering, this too was to be without defect.

"And if he bring a lamb for a sin offering, he shall bring it a female without blemish. And he shall lay his hand upon the head of the sin offering, and slay it for a sin offering in the place where they kill the burnt offering." Leviticus 4:32-33

These verses describe the sacrifice of a lamb and again the animal was to be without defect.

"And if he be not able to bring a lamb, then he shall bring for his trespass, which he hath committed, two turtledoves, or two young pigeons, unto the Lord; one for a sin offering, and the other for a burnt offering." Leviticus 5:7

Those who were too poor to be able to afford a larger animal, were permitted to offer turtledoves instead. Imagine you went to a marketplace and there you found an array of bulls and lambs on sale, but then you came across someone squatted in a corner trying to sell a few doves. Wouldn't this be a sad sight?

Even today if you go to a marketplace, you will find all kinds of merchandise on sale and sometimes you will come across someone tucked away in a corner trying to sell a few puppies, rabbits, or kittens. It seems that in the temple, too, where the sacrificial animals were on sale, there was someone who had brought along a few well-chosen doves.

What did Jesus say to these people who were selling the doves?

"Take these things hence." If I were a literary man, I would be able to depict this scene much more vividly, but since this is not where my talent lies, I must leave it to your imagination.

Destroy This Temple

Why did Jesus behave like this in the temple? Did He do it simply in order to cause a disturbance? That was definitely not the case at all.

> "And his disciples remembered that it was written, The zeal of thine house hath eaten me up."
> John 2:17

The words, "The zeal of thine house hath eaten me up," appear in Psalm 69 verse 9, but what does this mean? Jesus was cleaning out the temple that was being defiled by these people as they bought and sold their sacrificial animals. They gave the appearance of worshiping God, but their thoughts and hearts lay elsewhere and therefore they were defiling the temple that was there, symbolizing Christ.

> "Then answered the Jews and said unto him, What sign shewest thou unto us, seeing that thou doest these things?"
> John 2:18

The Jews asked Jesus for some kind of sign. They wanted evidence that would justify His actions. Let's think about this scene. It had taken 46 years to construct this huge and magnificent temple of which they were so proud and where they believed they worshiped God, but now Jesus had suddenly turned up and shaken everything to the core. There was utter confusion, the animals running havoc, bleating and mooing as they were driven out. So the Jews asked Jesus, "What sign shewest thou unto us?"

> "Jesus answered and said unto them, Destroy this temple, and in three days I will raise it up." John 2:19

Jesus said to them, "Destroy this temple, and in three days I will raise it up." Why do you think He said this? The Jews had built a very impressive temple of gold and silver, but an even better temple, a more holy temple than had been hoped for by all the Jews put together, was being accomplished in Jesus Himself. It was because Jesus had to die and then rise again from the dead in order that this temple might be completed that He said, "Destroy this temple."

The Jews, however, had no idea why Jesus made such a monstrous statement. They had read and studied the Old Testament scriptures and offered sacrifices in accordance with the Law, but they still did not know what Jesus meant when He said that He was going to die. They did not even understand when Jesus was nailed to the cross and died. His disciples could not even understand. It was only after He had risen from the dead and the Holy Spirit had come to them that they realized. Until then, no one understood, no matter how well they might have known the Old Testament scriptures.

Jesus said, "Destroy this temple." Let's consider these words. There is a huge difference between, "Destroy this temple," and "I will destroy this temple." In a court of law it often happens that false witnesses prevail. People who present such deceitful evidence are extremely audacious. They speak up with a loud voice, perhaps even unaware that this is perjury. This is what happened at Jesus' trial. When the Jews arrested Jesus and brought Him to trial, people brought false accusations against Him, claiming that he had said He would destroy the temple and then build it up again in three days.

> "And there arose certain, and bare false witness against him, saying, We heard him say, I will destroy this temple that is made with hands, and within three days I will build another made without hands."
>
> Mark 14:57-58

The false witnesses claimed that Jesus had said, "I will destroy this temple," when in fact He had said, "Destroy this temple." Let's take a look now at a passage in Matthew's Gospel.

> "But found none: yea, though many false witnesses came, yet found they none. At the last came two false witnesses, And said, This fellow said, I am able to destroy the temple of God, and to build it in three days."
>
> Matthew 26:60-61

Who did these people say had announced that he was going to destroy the temple? They quoted Jesus as having said, "I am able to destroy the temple of God and to rebuild it in three days." Were they telling the truth? It is very clear that they were lying.

If we do not read the Bible carefully, we may easily think that these false witnesses were justified in what they said. This, however, is not the case. Jesus said very clearly, "Destroy this temple." When He said this, He was telling them to put Him to death. If He had said, "I will destroy this temple and in three days I will raise it up," He would have been announcing that He was going to commit suicide and rise from the dead three days later. He actually said, "Destroy this temple, and in three days I will raise it up."

In Three Days I Will Raise It Up

Jesus knew what was going to happen to him in the future upon His third visit to Jerusalem for the Feast of the Passover. He also knew that His body was the temple in which the Holy Spirit dwelt. He knew all about the death that was to come to Him. All the sacrifices that the Jews had offered in the temple, all the bulls and other animals that had been slaughtered in this way, over the past 1,400 years, culminated in the death of Christ. Now, the hidden meaning behind all these ceremonies would be made clear. Jesus would be revealed as the perfect Lamb of God. This is why Jesus said, "Destroy this temple."

He was not telling them to destroy the temple building that had taken 46 years to construct. His own body was the temple and He was telling them to kill Him and in three days He would rise from the dead.

> "Jesus answered and said unto them, Destroy this temple, and in three days I will raise it up."   John 2:19

Jesus was talking here about His resurrection. Three days after He was killed, He rose from the dead. Only then was everything accomplished.

> "Then said the Jews, Forty and six years was this temple in building, and wilt thou rear it up in three days?"   John 2:20

Was this Man claiming that He would reconstruct in three days, a temple that had originally taken 46 years to build? Jesus' remark must have seemed preposterous to the Jews, and there would have been quite a commotion amongst them. All their thoughts were focused on the temple and everything connected with it. To them, the greatest sin was the sin of defiling the temple, and yet their temple was merely a shadow of Jesus. Everything involved in the preparations for the advent of the Christ was brought to fruition with the coming of Jesus. The true temple had now come and would be built up again three days after it had been destroyed, in other words, three days after Jesus had been crucified. Jesus' physical body that was in the form of the body of Adam had to be destroyed in order that the perfect body—the Church—might be established.

> "And the Word was made flesh, and dwelt among us, (and we beheld his glory, the glory as of the only begotten of the Father,) full of grace and truth." John 1:14

From this verse we can see that the Holy Spirit dwelt in all fullness in Jesus. In several verses in John's Gospel we find Jesus promising that after He had risen from the dead and ascended into heaven, He would send the Holy Spirit. In other words, three days after His crucifixion and death, He would be resurrected and the temple would be established in which the Holy Spirit would abide. This temple is the body of Jesus as referred to in Hebrews chapter 10 verse 5 where it says, "Sacrifice and offering thou wouldest not, but a body hast thou prepared me." After Jesus rose from the dead, He would become the head of the Church; the cornerstone and foundation of the spiritual temple of God. One by one, the believers are the stones that are being built up one upon another in Christ to form this temple. So in the letter to the Ephesians it says that the believers fitly framed together grow into a holy temple in the Lord.[10]

Jesus said to the merchants in the temple, "It is written, My house is the house of prayer: but ye have made it a den of thieves" Luke 19:46. This temple made with human hands was only a shadow and therefore it was no longer meaningful. The true holy temple was about to be established.

> "And are built upon the foundation of the apostles and prophets, Jesus Christ himself being the chief corner stone." Ephesians 2:20

What was the perfect foundation that was indicated by the apostles and the prophets? It was Christ. The Old Testament was pointing ahead to Christ and the New Testament bore witness of Him. Through the words of the New Testament recorded by the Holy Spirit through the apostles, we come to know Jesus as He appears in the Old Testament.

> "In whom all the building fitly framed together groweth unto an holy temple in the Lord: In whom ye also are builded together for an habitation of God through the Spirit." Ephesians 2:21-22

We, too, are being built up upon Christ, into a holy temple. In terms of a building, He is the cornerstone.

> "Now ye are the body of Christ, and members in particular." 1 Corinthians 12:27

It talks here of the body of Christ, but who is the head of that body? It is Jesus Christ, and we are the members of the body.

> "For as the body is one, and hath many members, and all the members of that one body, being many, are one body: so also is Christ." 1 Corinthians 12:12

In this verse it says that all the believers are members of the body of Christ. When it comes to the temple, Jesus is the foundation and the cornerstone, and we are the stones that are being built up upon it.

> "And he is the head of the body, the church: who is the beginning, the firstborn from the dead; that in all things he might have the preeminence." Colossians 1:18

"He," in this verse, is the head of the body that is the Church. At the time of Jesus, however, the Jews were paying no attention to the head, but carrying on their own business, treating the temple as a market place. Such is a temple made by the hands of men.

> "And not holding the Head, from which all the body by joints and bands having nourishment ministered, and knit together, increaseth with the increase of God." Colossians 2:19

Who is meant here by the Head? Christ is the Head and the believers are the members of the body. Through the head, we all become parts of the body. This is the way in which the temple is being accomplished, and this temple is alive and it is the dwelling place of the Holy Spirit.

The Power of Jesus' Name

> "But he spake of the temple of his body. When therefore he was risen from the dead, his disciples remembered that he had said this unto them; and they believed the scripture, and the word which Jesus had said." John 2:21-22

Jesus was talking about the temple of His body, but how could the disciples possibly have understood this? The Bible tells us that "they understood none of these things: and this saying was hid from them, neither knew they the things which were spoken" Luke 18:34. The disciples were only able to understand later when Jesus had risen from the dead and ascended into heaven and the Holy Spirit had come.

> Oh, spread the tidings round, wherever man is found,
> Wherever human hearts and human woes abound;
> Let every Christian tongue proclaim the joyful sound;
> The Comforter has come![11]

The Holy Spirit had come. Without the help of the Holy Spirit we would be able to get no further than vaguely assuming that the Bible message must be true. This is very different from coming to a firm belief.

> "When therefore he was risen from the dead, his disciples remembered that he had said this unto them; and they believed the scripture, and the word which Jesus had said." John 2:22

The scripture referred to here is the Old Testament. It was only when the One written of in the Old Testament rose from the dead that the disciples truly believed in Him and knew who He was. What would have happened if Jesus had not risen from the dead? There is nothing in this world in which we can believe.

An old Korean saying tells us that when a man dies he leaves behind his name and when a tiger dies it leaves behind its skin. But how many people actually leave behind their names? The names of most of the people who have lived in this world have just faded away in the past. Even those names engraved on tombstones crumble and fade. They may seem great at one time, but they all come to an end.

There is one Man, however, whose name still remains truly great even though He lived such a long time ago. He only lived to the age of 33, but has there ever been any name greater than His? Have you ever heard of a name greater than that of Jesus? If someone were to go out on to a crowded street and shout out the name of Socrates, Caesar, or even Clinton, most people would probably take no notice at all. If, however, someone walks through a crowd shouting out the name of Jesus, all the people in the crowd tend to recoil from him. Whether it is a crazy person who shouts out the name of Jesus, or someone in his right mind, people's thoughts towards that person will change. There's something in that name that brings about a reaction, although people generally do not know what it is. So it is that we sing hymns like, "All Hail the Power of Jesus' Name."[12]

If Jesus had not been crucified, if He had not died, but had instead lived a long and genteel life, there would be no sense in my standing up and preaching. He only lived for a short time, but what would become of us if each of our names were not covered by His? We would all end up in hell.

> For there's a new name written down in glory,
> And it's mine, O yes, it's mine!
> With my sins forgiven I am bound for Heaven,
> Never more to roam.[13]

"There's a new name written down in glory." When you go to heaven, how will you find your name has been recorded there? Will there be a list of names: John Smith, Mary Jones, Tom Brown…? In God's eyes, all of us are covered with all kinds of sins, but He has promised that when He looks at us and sees the blood, He will pass over us.[14]

Whose blood is this? It is the blood of Jesus. God has promised that when He sees this holy blood, He will pass over us. Thus we are forgiven through the name of Jesus. The kingdom of God is not so very complicated. It makes no difference whether our names are Smith, Jones, Brown, or whatever else they may be; it is through the name of Jesus that we enter the kingdom of God. We have this great name to back us up.

He Knew What Was in Man

> "Now when he was in Jerusalem at the passover, in the feast day, many believed in his name, when they saw the miracles which he did."
>
> John 2:23

Jesus was in Jerusalem during the Feast of the Passover and at that time many people believed in Him when they observed His deeds and the miracles He performed. He accomplished many works so that many believed in Him but He did not entrust Himself to any of them because He knew what was in their hearts. Let's take a brief look at what is inside the hearts of men.

Jesus had twelve disciples. One day the mother of two of these disciples approached Jesus and said, "Grant that these my two sons may sit, the one on thy right hand, and the other on the left, in thy kingdom" Matthew 20:21. This was a preposterous thing to suggest. When the other disciples heard this, they were furious and then they began to argue about who was the greatest among them.

Jesus, however, could see inside the hearts of everyone. He could see everything. At the end, He even said to His disciples, "All ye shall be offended because of me this night" Mark 14:27. He knew that all His disciples would forsake Him when He was arrested and crucified. When Peter heard this, he insisted that he would never desert Jesus. It was Peter's nature to be hasty in word and deed. He was a powerful man of action. Had he been a little more refined, he might have shown more self-restraint and just thought to himself, "No, Lord. I will never forsake You. You will see." But Peter just blurted out:

"Although all shall be offended, yet will not I."   Mark 14:29

Not only did he make such a rash declaration, but at the same time he also implicated everyone else. Such was Peter's display of audacity.

On the night of Jesus' arrest and interrogation, however, Peter only followed Jesus quietly at a distance and warmed himself by the fire in the courtyard outside. Then, when a woman approached him and said, "This man was also with Jesus," Peter flatly denied it, saying,

"I know not this man of whom ye speak" Mark 14:70. If Peter had been a little better educated, he might have said something like, "You can say what you like, but I know what I know." He could have let the situation pass in this way without incident, but in his rashness, Peter was just as quick to deny Jesus three times as he had been to declare his loyalty earlier. Just then, the cock crowed and the moment Peter heard it, he went out and wept bitterly. This was the way Peter was, and he could do nothing about it. Jesus knew all that was inside of these people and so it was that He could not entrust Himself to any person.

On another occasion, a large multitude of people were gathered around Jesus and he fed them all with just five loaves and two fishes. After that, the crowd continued to follow Him, thinking that if they made Him their king, they would never starve. They did not believe in the Christ who had come to fulfil the Old Testament by dying on the cross and rising from the dead three days later; they followed Jesus because they were impressed by the miracles He performed. But for these people at that point in time, He could become neither their king, their head, nor their cornerstone. He had already overcome this temptation when approached by the devil right at the beginning of His ministry. So Jesus said:

> "And Jesus said unto him, Foxes have holes, and birds of the air have nests; but the Son of man hath not where to lay his head." Luke 9:58

Jesus once referred to Herod as a fox. He said, "Go ye, and tell that fox, Behold, I cast out devils, and I do cures to day and to morrow, and the third day I shall be perfected" Luke 13:32. He also said, "The birds of the air have their nests" Matthew 8:20. The birds of the air symbolize the devil who enters the hearts of men. Also, in the parable of the sower, Jesus said, "Some seeds fell by the way side, and the fowls came and devoured them up" Matthew 13:4.

These birds symbolize the devil who comes and snatches away God's word from those who try to receive it. This happens now as it did also at the time of Jesus.

> "But Jesus did not commit himself unto them, because he knew all men, And needed not that any should testify of man: for he knew what was in man."
> John 2:24-25

No matter how great, pure, and righteous a person may appear to be, God knows what is in man's heart since He created man. This is because God's lamp is alight in the heart of each individual.

> "The spirit of man is the candle of the Lord, searching all the inward parts of the belly."
> Proverbs 20:27

Jesus knew man completely, but He had not yet become the head of the Church or its cornerstone, so it says that He did not entrust Himself to anyone.

Let us pray.

Lord God, we truly thank You. We know that we live the whole of our humble lowly lives weighed down by hearts that are full of greed, but You have given mankind Your word, which sets man free from all the chains that bind him, and for this we truly thank You. Lord, we pray that, for as long as we are living on this earth, Your holy word that You have entrusted to us will be the light of our lives and will spread out to the world through us. We pray also that You will help us so that we may discover the work that we are to do and be able to be Your true witnesses through that work. Lord, rouse us to this work. We pray that the Holy Spirit will fill all that is lacking in each one of us, and that You will take control of the rest of our lives and our thoughts. We pray in the name of the Lord Jesus, Amen.

◆ Notes

Chapter 1
[1] "How Great Thou Art!," Carl Boberg (1859-1940).
[2] "The Love of God," Frederick M. Lehman (1868-1953).
[3] "All Creatures of Our God and King," Francis of Assisi (1181-1226).

Chapter 2
[1] "Alas! and Did My Saviour Bleed," Isaac Watts (1674-1748).
[2] It is recorded in the Bible that it is not God's intention that man dies without obtaining eternal life.

"He keepeth back his soul from the pit, and his life from perishing by the sword." Job 33:18

"Thou hast in love to my soul delivered it from the pit of corruption: for thou hast cast all my sins behind thy back." Isaiah 38:17

"As I live, saith the Lord God, I have no pleasure in the death of the wicked; but that the wicked turn from his way and live." Ezekiel 33:11

"Even so it is not the will of your Father which is in heaven, that one of these little ones should perish." Matthew 18:14

"And this is the Father's will which hath sent me, that of all which he hath given me I should lose nothing, but should raise it up again at the last day." John 6:39

[3] "Majestic Sweetness Sits Enthroned," Samuel Stennett (1727-1795).
[4] "O Happy Day," Philip Doddridge (1702-1751).
[5] "Brightly Beams Our Father's Mercy," Philip Paul Bliss (1838-1876).
[6] "What a Wonderful Change," Rufus Henry McDaniel (1850-1940).

Chapter 3
[1] A talent is a unit of money worth 3,000 shekels or 6,000 denarii. One denaruis was equivalent to one day's wage. In terms of weight, a talent was probably about 75 lbs (34 kg).

2 "The Love of God is Greater Far," Frederick Martin Lehman (1868-1953).

3 "Christ" (Greek) and "Messiah" (Hebrew) mean "the anointed one."

4 Matthew chapter 22 verse 15 and Mark chapter 12 verse 13 refer to the Pharisees and the Herodians, while Luke chapter 20 verse 19 refers to the chief priests and scribes. The positions of chief priests at that time had been secured by the Sadducees, so it is presumed that these three powers joined forces to try to force Jesus into a trap.

5 The Romans periodically carried out population censuses in order to facilitate collection of taxes and enlist soldiers. Since the Jews were exempt from the Roman army, in their case a census was carried out purely in order to enable efficient collection of taxes.

6 At that time, the denarius was the silver coin used when paying taxes. The Roman emperor at the time Jesus said these words was Tiberius, so the image of this emperor would probably have been inscribed on the coin.

7 "What a Wonderful Change," Rufus Henry McDaniel (1850-1940)

8 Herodias was the daughter of Aristobulus, the son of Herod the Great. She married Herod Philip, her uncle, by whom she had a daughter, Salome. Then she accepted the advances of her husband's half brother, Herod Antipas, who was Tetrarch of Galilee. In order to be able to marry Herodias, Herod Antipas divorced his wife, Phasaelis - daughter of Aretas IV, king in Arabia. John the Baptist was imprisoned for criticizing Herod for this immoral union. Herodias detested John the Baptist for his criticisms, so when her daughter pleased King Herod with her dancing on his birthday, she told her daughter to demand the head of John the Baptist. Later the Roman emperor comanded that Herod Antipas and Herodias be sent into exile.

9 "Hail to the Brightness of Zion's Glad Morning," Thomas Hastings (1784-1872).

10 "In the Rifted Rock I'm Resting," Mary D. Jones (1810-1883).

Chapter 4
1 See Luke 3:10-14.
2 See John 1:9-11.

3 "Christ, thy Lord is Waiting Now," Franklin Sheppard (1852-1930).

4 "I Can Sing Now the Song," Russell Kelso Carter (1849-1928).

5 "The Path Without the Camp," Gospel Hymnal.

6 "Jesus Comes With Pow'r to Gladden," Carrie Breck (1855-1934).

7 In those days in Israel, time was calculated by dividing the day into twelve hours, from sunrise to sunset. The hour of sunrise was the first hour and the hour of sunset the twelfth hour. The first hour is roughly equivalent to our 6 or 7 o'clock a.m., and the twelfth hour to 5 or 6 p.m.

8 "'Tis so Sweet to Walk With Jesus," Albert Simpson (1843-1919).

9 "I'm Rejoicing Night and Day," Herbert Buffum (1879-1939).

Chapter 5

1 "I Can Hear My Savior Calling," Earnest W. Blandy.

2 "O Happy Day, That Fixed My Choice," Philip Doddridge (1702-1751).

3 "I Know Not Why God's Wondrous Grace," Daniel Webster Whittle (1840-1901).

4 Some people have conjectured that Nathanael and Jesus' disciple Bartholomew are the same person.

5 The northern region of Galilee was surrounded on three sides by gentile lands and heavily populated by gentiles, including the native Canaanites. The Law was less strictly adhered to among the Jews in this region, and intermarriage between Jews and gentiles was prevalent. Consequently, the racially pure and law-abiding Jews in Judea in the south scorned the inhabitants of Galilee. Nazareth, in which Jesus was raised, was a town in Galilee.

6 In 586 BC, Judea was captured by Babylon. About 70 years later, in 515 BC, the Jews returned to their homeland and completed the second temple, the temple of Zerubbabel. They were not, however, able to restore Israel's nationhood. At the time of the birth of Jesus, Israel was under Roman rule. In 70 AD, Jerusalem was destroyed at the hands of the Roman general Titus, and the Jews were scattered all over the world. On May 14, 1948, Israel once again was declared an

independent nation, as had been prophesied in the Bible. In June 1967, Israel recaptured the city of Jerusalem, the temple, however, has yet to be restored to Israel.

[7] "The First Noel, The Angel Did Say," Traditional English Carol.

[8] See Micah 5:2.

[9] "We've a Story to Tell to the Nations," Henry Earnest Nichol (1862-1928).

[10] Although the word "tithe" is not used, the first record of tithing in the Bible appears in Genesis chapter 14. As Abraham made his return after rescuing his nephew Lot from the kings of Mesopotamia, he encountered the priest Melchizedek and offered him a tenth of all he had received.

[11] "O Happy Day, that Fixed My Choice," Philip Doddridge (1702-1751).

[12] "When the Trumpet of the Lord Shall Sound," James Milton Black (1856-1938).

[13] "Jesus, the Very Thought of Thee," Bernard of Clairvaux (1091-1153).

[14] "My Hope is Built on Nothing Less," Edward Mote (1797-1874).

Chapter 6

[1] See Exodus 5:3; 8:27.

[2] See Ecclesiastes chapter 3.

[3] "Fly as a Bird," Mary Stanley Schindler.

[4] "Jesus Has Shed His Precious Blood."

[5] "Old Folks at Home," Stephen Collins Foster.

[6] See also Mark 14:36; Luke 22:42.

Chapter 7

[1] The Passover is a feast celebrated in memory of the day on which the Israelites were saved from their bondage in Egypt. Exodus chapter 12 verse 13 explains the origin of the Passover: And the blood shall be a sign for you on the houses where you live; and when I see the blood I will pass over you, and no plague will befall you to destroy you when I

strike the land of Egypt. The Jews first celebrated the Passover in approximately 1447 BC. See Exodus chapter 12; Exodus 8:25-32; Deuteronomy chapter 16.

[2] See 1 Corinthians 5:7.

[3] "Christ Our Redeemer," John G. Foote.

[4] See Luke 24:44-45.

[5] The History of the Temple

The tabernacle was built according to God's instructions after the Israelites had come out of Egypt. Since the entire nation of the Jews was on the move at that time, the tabernacle was designed so that it could easily be transported and re-assembled. Inside the tabernacle was the Ark of the Covenant, which housed the stone tablets on which the Ten Commandments were inscribed.

Solomon's Temple. Some time after the Israelites settled in the land of Canaan, King David became concerned because the Ark of God was kept in the tent-like structure of the tabernacle while he himself lived in a royal palace. He therefore made up his mind to construct a temple building. Following a revelation from God, David drew up the plans of the temple and the utensils to be used in the temple. Before he died, he handed over these plans to Solomon, his son. Later Solomon took seven years to complete this temple, which is referred to as Solomon's Temple.

Zerubbabel's Temple. During the Babylonian invasion of Israel, Solomon's temple was destroyed and the Israelites were taken captive to Babylon. Seventy years later, the Israelites returned to their land. It was then that Zerubbabel, who had been appointed governor of Judea, and Jeshua, the priest, were key figures in reconstructing the destroyed temple. This temple is also referred to as the Second Temple.

Herod's Temple. King Herod was an Idumean who ruled over Jerusalem at the time of the birth of Jesus. In order to win the favor of the Jews, Herod had Zerubbabel's Temple restored, a feat that took 46 years. Being a gentile, however, Herod himself was not permitted to enter the temple.

The Third Temple. The temple in Jerusalem was completely destroyed in 70 AD, but it will be built again during the last days of this world. It is there that the antichrist will make himself out to be God.

6 See Numbers 9:12.

7 See 1 Peter 1:19.

8 The Veil

While the Israelites were in the wilderness, there were two veils in the tabernacle. One hung at the entrance to the tabernacle, and the other between the Holy Place and the Most Holy. As Jesus died on the cross, this latter veil tore from top to bottom. See Matthew 27:51. This veil was made of linen woven from blue, purple, and scarlet thread. Cherubim were elaborately embroidered onto the veil. The Israelites hung this veil inside the tabernacle on four pillars of shittim wood. See Exodus 26:31-33; 2 Chronicles 3:14. When the Israelites moved the tabernacle in the course of their travels, they took down this veil and covered the ark with it. See Numbers 4:5. No one except the chief priest was allowed to go behind the veil into the Most Holy Place. Even the chief priest could only go there once a year on the Day of Atonement. See Hebrews 9:7. It was because the Most Holy Place was the place where God dwelt that it was cordoned off by the veil. When the veil that blocked the way between man and God was torn, the way was opened for everyone to draw near to God through Christ.

9 See Ephesians 2:21.

10 "O Spread the Tidings Round," Francis Bottome (1823-1894).

11 "All Hail the Power of Jesus' Name," Edward Perronet (1726-1792).

12 "A New Name in Glory," Charles Austin Miles (1874-1948).

13 See Exodus 12:13.